110662033

GAINING
A FRESH
PERSPECTIVE

Seeing Relationships

through New Eyes

From the Bible-Teaching Ministry of

Charles R. Swindoll

INSIGHT *for* LIVING

Insight for Living's Bible teacher, Chuck Swindoll, has devoted his life to the clear, practical application of God's Word and His grace. A pastor at heart, Chuck has served as senior pastor to congregations in Texas, Massachusetts, and California. He currently leads Stonebriar Community Church in Frisco, Texas, but Chuck's listening audience extends far beyond a local church body. As a leading program in Christian broadcasting, *Insight for Living* airs in major Christian radio markets, through more than 2,100 outlets worldwide, in 16 languages, and to a growing webcast audience. Chuck's extensive writing ministry has also served the body of Christ worldwide, and his leadership as president and now chancellor of Dallas Theological Seminary has helped prepare and equip a new generation for ministry. Chuck and Cynthia, his partner in life and ministry, have four grown children and ten grandchildren.

Based on the outlines, charts, and transcripts of Charles R. Swindoll's sermons, the study guide text was developed and written by the creative ministries department of Insight for Living.

Editor in Chief:
Cynthia Swindoll

Study Guide Writer:
Marla Alupoaicei
Brian Goins

Senior Editor and Assistant Writer:
Marla Alupoaicei

Editor:
Amy LaFuria

Typesetter:
Bob Haskins

Rights and Permissions:
The Meredith Agency

Unless otherwise identified, all Scripture references are from the New American Standard Bible © The Lockman Foundation 1960, 1962, 1963, 1968, 1971, 1972, 1973, 1975, 1977, 1995. Used by permission.

Copyright © 2002 by Insight for Living. All rights reserved.

Original outlines, charts, and transcripts:
Copyright © 2002 by Charles R. Swindoll. All rights reserved.

An effort has been made to locate sources and obtain permission where necessary for the quotations used in this book. In the event of any unintentional omission, a modification will gladly be incorporated in future printings.

NOTICE: All rights reserved under international copyright conventions. No part of this book may be reproduced in any form or by any means, electronic or mechanical, including photocopying, recording, or by any information storage and retrieval system, without permission in writing from the publisher. Inquiries should be addressed to Insight for Living, Rights and Permissions, Post Office Box 251007, Plano, Texas, 75025-1007. The Rights and Permissions department can also be reached by e-mail at rights@insight.org.

ISBN 1-57972-442-6
Cover design: Robert Page and Associates
Cover image: Arni Katz/Index Stock Imagery, Inc.
Printed in the United States of America

CONTENTS

INTRODUCTION

Few things try my patience more than a traffic jam. You jump on the freeway only to find a parking lot. You see an exit ahead. Do you chance an alternate route or stay in gridlock hoping the dam breaks? You're stuck. If only you could hop in a helicopter and hover above the fray for just a glimpse of what's ahead. You need a fresh perspective.

Similarly, many people are "stuck" in their relationships. Grudges grind friendships to a halt. Bitterness congests marriages. Neighbors share fences but stifle conversation. Even churches clog up with strained relationships brought on by faulty perceptions and misguided intentions. If only we could hop on the back of an angel, hover above the mess, and discover God's preferred route. Again, we need a fresh perspective.

In this study, we want to look at our relationships with new eyes. Cruising through passages in Joel, the Gospels, Acts, and Romans, we want to gain God's perspective on our most valued relationships. If you're tired of moving at a snail's pace, feel like too much of your past is too full of regret, or you're simply looking for God's divine path to get you through the latest relational "jam," you're holding the answer in your hands. This study will help you gain the fresh perspective you've been looking for.

Chuck Swindoll

Charles R. Swindoll

PUTTING TRUTH
INTO ACTION

Knowledge apart from application falls short of God's desire for His children. He wants us to apply what we learn so that we will change and grow. This Bible study guide was prepared with these goals in mind. As you go through the following pages, we hope your desire to discover biblical truth will grow as your understanding of God's Word increases and that you will be encouraged to apply what you've learned.

To assist you in your study, we've included a section called 🌸 **Living Insights** at the end of each lesson. These exercises will challenge you to study further and to think of specific ways to put your discoveries into action.

There are many ways to use this guide—in personal devotions, group studies, discussions with friends and family, and Sunday school classes. And, of course, it's an ideal study aid when you're listening to its corresponding *Insight for Living* radio series.

To benefit most from this Bible study guide, we encourage you to consider it a spiritual journal. That's why we've included space in the Living Insights for recording your thoughts and discoveries. We hope you'll return to those sections often for review and encouragement as you continue to grow in your walk with Christ.

Insight for Living

GAINING
A FRESH
PERSPECTIVE

Chapter 1

LOOKING BACK: CLEARING AWAY THE TRASH WE REGRET

Joel 1:2–20; 2:12–27

New Year's resolutions—we all make them. Unfortunately, they too often turn into New Year's dissolutions by the second week of January. Our unrealistic expectations quickly transform into frustration over our unmet goals.

Columnist Dave Barry offers the following parody of our annual proclamations:

> Be realistic. Many people give up because they "set their sights too high." In making a New Year's resolution, pick a goal that you can reasonably expect to attain, as we see in these examples:
>
> Unrealistic Goal: "In the next month, I will lose 25 pounds."
> Realistic Goal: "Over the next year, taking it an ounce or two at a time, I will gain 25 pounds, and my face will bloat like a military life raft."
>
> Unrealistic Goal: "I will learn to speak Chinese."
> Realistic Goal: "I will order some Chinese food."
>
> Unrealistic Goal: "I will read a good book."
> Realistic Goal: "I will examine the outsides of some good books, then waddle over to the part of the bookstore where they sell pastries."[1]

---

1. Dave Barry, "Resolve to Be the Best Person You Can in '98—Someone Else," *The Sacramento (Calif.) Bee*, Jan. 4, 1998.

1

In our spiritual lives, we tend to make similar grandiose claims, such as: "This year, I will not yell at my kids," or "This year, I will lead everyone in my neighborhood to Christ," or perhaps, "This year, our marriage will recapture the romance of its youth." And some of us have given up on resolutions altogether. It simply hurts too much when we fail.

In this study we will attempt the unthinkable—to make resolutions and actually keep them. We aim to echo the words of Asaph when he exhorted, "Make vows to the Lord, *and keep them*" (Psalm 76:11, emphasis added). What a concept! So basic. So simple. And yet so perplexing.

Why do we have so much trouble keeping our resolutions? Because we often try to step towards the future without first addressing the past. If you have ever taken a driver's education class, you may remember your instructor reminding you, "Check the rearview mirror!" before you stepped on the gas. Before we go forward or change lanes, we need to make sure the road is clear behind us.

The process of addressing the past naturally brings with it pain and discomfort. The "driving records" of our lives are blemished by mistakes, wrong turns, a few fender benders, and probably even a major accident or two. We've most likely seen a few loved ones get hurt along the way. And undoubtedly, our records are marked by some regrets. Most of the time, rather than dealing with these failures and disappointments, we'd prefer to leave the past behind and put the pedal to the metal!

Our sin continues to have consequences even long afterwards. The Israelites experienced these consequences firsthand. During the time of the prophet Joel, God's chosen people repeatedly ignored Him and incurred painful punishment as a result of their transgressions. They found themselves reeling from the devastation as their rebellion against the Lord resulted in three successive natural disasters.

After each catastrophe, the nation tried to simply press on by making new resolutions to rebuild. But the prophet Joel, whose name meant "Yahweh is God," exhorted Israel to address her past and repent of her sins. His exhortations remind us to "Check the rearview mirror!" before pressing on into the future.

Depiction of the Devastation

Picture coming home for dinner and finding only ashes where your house once stood. Then imagine all your assets drying up at the bank before you could make a withdrawal. Finally, picture a powerful tornado wiping out your town, leaving nothing but splintered wood and bare fields.

Welcome to the land of Israel in the age of the prophets!

The first chapter of Joel chronicles the destruction inflicted upon the southern kingdom by three natural disasters. First, fire consumed the once-lush forests:

> To You, O Lord, I cry;
> For fire has devoured the pastures of the wilderness
> And the flame has burned up all the trees of the
>   field. (Joel 1:19)

Secondly, a severe drought drained all the brooks:

> Even the beasts of the field pant for You;
> For the water brooks are dried up
> And fire has devoured the pastures of the wilderness.
> (v. 20)

Lastly, an army of locusts devoured everything green:

> What the gnawing locust has left, the swarming
>   locust has eaten;
> And what the swarming locust has left, the creeping
>   locust has eaten;
> And what the creeping locust has left, the stripping
>   locust has eaten.
> Awake, drunkards, and weep;
> And wail, all you wine drinkers,
> On account of the sweet wine
> That is cut off from your mouth.
> For a nation has invaded my land,
> Mighty and without number;
> Its teeth are the teeth of a lion,
> And it has the fangs of a lioness.
> It has made my vine a waste
> And my fig tree splinters.
> It has stripped them bare and cast them away;
> Their branches have become white. (vv. 4–7)

Each of these plagues was devastating. But the locust plague dealt a blow to the economy of the ancient Near East rivaling that of America's Great Stock Market Crash of 1929. One day's devastation

3

resulted in a generation's disaster. The results of years of backbreaking plowing, planting, fertilizing, watering, and tilling vanished as if the work was never done. The people could do nothing to hold back the advancing swarm of locusts as it swept suddenly through the region of Judah.

The prophet Joel illustrated how the waves of locusts attacked. First came the "gnawing locusts" to clear out the vegetation. Whatever the "gnawing locusts" left, the "swarming locusts" consumed. Then the "creeping locusts," which had no wings, picked up anything left on the ground. Finally, the "stripping locusts" pulled off all the bark from the trees and the shoots from the plants. Once the locusts had finished their work, Israel's crops, plants, and trees resembled broomsticks. Without shedding any blood, the locusts had destroyed a nation's hope—along with its food supply.

In 1915, locusts invaded Palestine once more. John D. Whiting, a correspondent for *National Geographic*, described the devastation using terms similar to Joel's:

> Once entering a vineyard the sprawling vines would in the shortest time be nothing but bare bark. When the daintier morsels were gone, the bark was eaten off the young topmost branches, which, after exposure to the sun, were bleached snow-white. Then, seemingly out of malice, they would gnaw off small limbs, perhaps to get at the pith within . . . They stripped every leaf, berry, and even the tender bark . . . Even on the scarce and prized palms they had no pity, gnawing off the tenderer ends of the sword-like branches and, diving deep into the heart, they tunneled after the juicy pith.[2]

Maybe you feel like a once-fruitful plant attacked by locusts. What was once growing and blossoming in your life has withered on the vine. Consequences from past sins have swooped in and feasted on your soul, and all that remains is regret. On the surface, things may look the same—you dress fashionably, go to work, say the right words, and go through the motions—but your outlook on life reveals the emptiness you feel.

---

2. John D. Whiting, as quoted by James Montgomery Boice in *The Minor Prophets: Two Volumes Complete in One Edition* (Grand Rapids, Mich.: Kregel Publications, 1996), p. 102.

Poet and author John Greenleaf Whittier once wrote, "For all sad words of tongue or pen/The saddest are these: 'It might have been!'"[3] Isn't it easy to dwell on what might have been? When our heads hit the pillow at night, we may be tempted to stare at the ceiling and mumble, "If I only . . . , I should have . . . , If I could have just . . ."? But *ifs* can't change the past.

Remorse can be defined as "a gnawing distress arising from a sense of guilt for past wrongs."[4] We all feel remorse over words we shouldn't have spoken and sins we shouldn't have committed. So how do we deal with the past? Do we just ignore the devastation and press forward?

Divinely Designed Disaster

A disaster of this magnitude had never before struck the land of Judah. Before the Israelites could don their sandals and move on, Joel forced the people to pause and consider the seriousness of their transgressions:

> Hear this, O elders,
> And listen, all inhabitants of the land.
> Has anything like this happened in your days
> Or in your fathers' days?
> Tell your sons about it,
> And let your sons tell their sons,
> And their sons the next generation. (Joel 1:2–3)

The Lord was not finished yet. If Israel tried to simply pick up the pieces and press on without repenting, the people would face future devastation that would make the plague look like a picnic (Joel 2:1–11). But fortunately, the Lord sent the locusts.

Yes, you read that correctly! You might call it a divinely designed disaster. In Joel 2:25, God refers to the locusts as "My great army which I sent among you." The Lord had mustered these tiny locust "soldiers" into battle to achieve His divine purposes.

Why did God bring this plague upon Israel? The book of Hebrews states that God disciplines those He loves (12:4–11). We discipline our children not just to punish present transgressions, but

---

3. John Greenleaf Whittier, from the poem "Maud Muller," at http://www.princeton.edu/~ampayne/maud_muller.html, accessed on July 24, 2002.

4. *Merriam-Webster's Collegiate Dictionary*, 10th ed., see "remorse."

to prevent future character flaws. The Lord's goal was not to bring hurt and devastation but to call for repentance and bring about the restoration of a damaged relationship. When His people's hearts stopped longing for Him and instead desired the things of the world, God shocked their systems to help them regain a spiritual pulse.

Three Principles of Restoration

When we come to Joel 2, we discover a promise from Yahweh to the people of Israel:

> "Then I will make up to you for the years
> That the swarming locust has eaten,
> The creeping locust, the stripping locust and the
>   gnawing locust,
> My great army which I sent among you.
> You will have plenty to eat and be satisfied
> And praise the name of the Lord your God,
> Who has dealt wondrously with you;
> Then My people will never be put to shame.
> Thus you will know that I am in the midst of Israel,
> And that I am the Lord your God,
> And there is no other;
> And My people will never be put to shame."
> (Joel 2:25–27)

Though He punished them, God wanted His people to be restored. The words *make up* in verse 1 mean "to make whole or good, restore [a] thing lost."[5] Yahweh promised to replace ravaged crops, restore the economy, and reconcile His covenant relationship with Israel. In our day, He promises to repair ravaged lives, restore relationships, and revive hardened hearts. But before He clears away the trash and restores hope, we must play our part.

Notice that Joel 2:25 begins with the word *then*. Something preceded the Lord's promise. God required an action from Israel. Teaching the people three biblical principles of reconciliation through Joel, God offered the Israelites an opportunity to redeem the years stolen by the locusts. God offers us these same principles to clean away the years of regret and remorse that have built up in our lives.

---

5. Richard Whitaker, ed., *The Unabridged Brown-Driver-Briggs Hebrew-English Lexicon of the Old Testament,* accessed through the Logos Library System.

Start Immediately without Rationalization

When God confronted Adam about his sin, Adam tried to rationalize it by blaming Eve. She, in turn, blamed the serpent. In the same way, when we were young, if our parents caught us in a lie, we might have tried to defend our actions by saying, "The devil made me do it!"

Today, we simply dress up our rationalizations in better clothes: "It's just a little white lie," "I needed to protect this person," "Everyone else fudges a bit on their taxes," "I need to tell you about so-and-so, so you will be better informed about how to pray for him." But the words of the prophet Joel strip us of our excuses. They leave us with nothing but the plain truth. We've blown it! And we are to approach God with humble hearts:

> "Yet even now," declares the Lord,
> "Return to Me with all your heart,
> And with fasting, weeping and mourning;
> And rend your heart and not your garments."
> (Joel 2:12–13a)

Instead of saying, "The devil made me do it," we should be willing to say, "I am to blame." Instead of complaining, "But you don't understand the pressure I'm under!" we should accept responsibility and say, "It was my fault." We can't pass the buck; we can't shirk our responsibilities. We need to look at the wasteland brought about by our sins and point the finger in one direction—our own! And we need to do it immediately, because God desires a restored relationship and renewed intimacy with us as soon as possible. In His mercy, He wants to give us back those years that were lost to the locusts.

Return Completely without Reservation

God says to come back with "all your heart." He wants us to return to Him with humble hearts, confessing and repenting fully of our sins. Would you want to be operated on by a surgeon who decides to ignore a tumor because he or she doesn't want to bother you with the trouble? We call that malpractice! In the same way, God requires full disclosure of our sins in order for restoration and forgiveness to occur.

A common practice in the ancient Near East was the rending, or tearing, of garments to outwardly express sorrow.[6] But in Joel's

or tearing, of garments to outwardly express sorrow.[6] But in Joel's day, God desired more than just a superficial act; He wanted a rending of the heart. When our hearts break before a holy God, we may respond with fasting, weeping, and mourning. But we should resist putting on an emotional show without spiritual substance. Otherwise, people around us may be convinced of our sincerity, but the Lord despairs over our hypocrisy. Sincere expressions of worship must flow from true life-change.

Repent Openly without Hesitation

Finally, repent honestly and quickly. If the Spirit has pricked your heart, refuse to let the sun go down until you have listened to Him and obeyed His call without hesitation. The prophet Joel called the Israelites to do just this:

> Blow a trumpet in Zion,
> Consecrate a fast, proclaim a solemn assembly,
> Gather the people, sanctify the congregation,
> Assemble the elders,
> Gather the children and the nursing infants.
> Let the bridegroom come out of his room
> And the bride out of her bridal chamber.
> Let the priests, the Lord's ministers,
> Weep between the porch and the altar,
> And let them say, "Spare Your people, O Lord,
> And do not make Your inheritance a reproach,
> A byword among the nations.
> Why should they among the people say,
> 'Where is their God?'" (Joel 2:15–17)

Joel shouted out several urgent commands: Blow a trumpet! Consecrate a fast! Proclaim an assembly! Gather the people! Sanctify the congregation! Assemble the elders! He called everyone to the town square—young, old, and everything in between. Anxious newlyweds were even snatched away from their anticipated union.

But repentance couldn't wait! Joel illustrated that nothing was of higher priority than being sure one's slate was wiped clean before almighty God.

All too often we tell ourselves that we'll wait for the just the right moment to repent. But Joel exhorts us to initiate, not meditate. And

---

6. J. D. Douglas, *New Bible Dictionary* (Wheaton, Ill: Tyndale House, 1996), accessed through the Logos Library System.

this exhortation applies not only to our vertical relationship with God, but our horizontal relationships with people as well. If we have exasperated our children, demeaned our spouse, or broken faith with a coworker, we must take steps to mend the relationship. The clock is ticking, and the rift widens with every second that passes.

What's the first thing you are asked to do when you walk into a doctor's office? The receptionist asks for your insurance card and then gives you a lengthy questionnaire to find out if you have ever had any illnesses or injuries—from a heart attack to diabetes to a paper cut. Why? Because your doctor can't fully assess your symptoms, diagnose your illness, or prescribe medication until he or she first knows your medical history. Part of your diagnosis involves uncovering your past.

As you reflect upon your past and look with hope to the future, reflect upon this heartfelt prayer by the psalmist David:

"Search me, O God, and know my heart;
Try me and know my anxious thoughts;
And see if there be any hurtful way in me,
And lead me in the everlasting way."
(Psalm 139:23–24)

Ask the Lord to help you search out past wrongs—sinful words, attitudes, and actions that did not glorify Him. Ask for forgiveness from Him as well as from anyone you may have hurt along the way. Then, ask your heavenly Father to renew your heart. He promises to do just that! You must deal with your past and leave it behind in order for your future resolutions to succeed!

 Living Insights

When disaster strikes, it's common to assume that God is judging a person or group of people for their sin. For example, in the early 1980s, some tried to create a direct connection between homosexuality and the AIDS epidemic, claiming that God sent AIDS as a curse upon homosexuals for their sinful actions. But many people who contracted AIDS were not involved in the homosexual lifestyle at all, including innocent children and hemophiliacs who contracted the disease from blood transfusions. We should be careful not to assume that all seemingly negative circumstances are the result of God's punishment.

Jesus addressed this issue in Luke 13:1–5:

> Now on the same occasion there were some present who reported to Him about the Galileans whose blood Pilate had mixed with their sacrifices. And Jesus said to them, "Do you suppose that these Galileans were greater sinners than all other Galileans because they suffered this fate? I tell you, no, but unless you repent, you will all likewise perish. Or do you suppose that those eighteen on whom the tower in Siloam fell and killed them were worse culprits than all the men who live in Jerusalem? I tell you, no, but unless you repent, you will all likewise perish."

How does Jesus rebuff these people's faulty logic?

_____

_____

_____

When tragedy strikes, to what response does Jesus call us?

_____

_____

One Bible scholar notes that when we read of such tragedies, we should ask: "'Why haven't these disasters come upon us? Why haven't they destroyed us?' Our problem is that we have forgotten how sinful we are. We have forgotten that it generally takes a disaster of unparalleled proportions to wake us from sin's lethargy."[7]

While God does not "send" judgments upon people in our times as He did in the Old Testament, He does allow circumstances and situations of testing to occur in order to sanctify and mature us in our faith. The next time a friend or loved one faces a difficult situation, instead of responding to the tragedy with blame or an attitude of prideful self-righteousness, remember that it could have happened to you. Respond to your loved ones with a gentle and humble spirit, as God uses you to encourage them.

7. James Montgomery Boice, *The Minor Prophets: Two Volumes Complete in One Edition* (Grand Rapids, Mich.: Kregel Publications, 1996), p. 105.

Chapter 2

LOOKING BACK:
FINDING HEALING
THROUGH FORGIVENESS

Matthew 5:23–24; 18:21–35

Bible scholar and author Philip Yancey calls forgiveness "an unnatural act."[1] We all know the difficulty of offering forgiveness to those who have hurt us. But if we stubbornly refuse to carry out this "unnatural act," we choose to remain in a state of "ungrace." According to Yancey:

> Ungrace causes cracks to fissure open between mother and daughter, father and son, brother and sister . . . and tribes, and races. Left alone, cracks widen, and for the resulting chasms of ungrace there is only one remedy: the frail rope-bridge of forgiveness.[2]

Our bodies and souls react as we take the first step onto this precarious, swaying rope-bridge. As memories of past pain flood our minds, we ask, *Why should I be the one to cross the chasm?* Often, we'd prefer to take out a long, sharp sword and cut down the bridge, leaving the abyss of unforgiveness forever uncrossed. But we are called to a ministry of reconciliation. As writer George Herbert stated, "He who cannot forgive another breaks the bridge over which he must pass himself."[3]

The curriculum of the Christian life requires a course in forgiveness. We all know from personal experience that this course's exams present some of life's most arduous challenges. Yet Scripture warns us that if we refuse to forgive others, we will receive the same refusal from our heavenly Father (see Matt. 18:21–35).

---

1. Philip Yancey, *What's So Amazing About Grace?* (Grand Rapids, Mich.: Zondervan Publishing House, 1997), p. 84.

2. Yancey, *What's So Amazing About Grace?*, p. 84.

3. George Herbert, as quoted by Philip Yancey in *What's So Amazing About Grace?*, p. 82.

Not only are we commanded to offer forgiveness to others, we're also called to humbly seek reconciliation for wrongs we have committed against them. In this chapter, we'll examine forgiveness from both sides of the chasm—from the perspective of those asking for it as well as from those granting it. What's our goal? To take care of the unfinished business in our past so we can begin to look ahead to a promising future.

Asking for Forgiveness

Without a worldwide radio broadcast, a tape ministry, or even a pulpit, a traveling Teacher named Jesus delivered the most-quoted sermon in all of history. The Gospel writer Matthew records this profound message that was shared with Christ's disciples on a lonely mountain in Galilee, the "Sermon on the Mount."

In this sermon, Jesus trumped the religiosity of pharisaical Judaism with His radical teaching on kingdom life. While the Pharisees reduced the Mosaic Law from a paradigm for a lifestyle of worship to a nitpicky set of rules, Jesus revealed the heart of the Father by focusing on God's true law. In Matthew 5, He taught several vital lessons on personal relationships.

In a series of "You have heard that it was said" propositions, Jesus elevated true worship over a falsely pious show of righteousness (see vv. 21, 27, 33, 38, 43). While the Law stated, "Thou shalt not murder," Jesus informed the disciples that those who harbor angry, hateful thoughts fall into the same category with those who commit murder! He dramatically demonstrated that it *is* the thought that counts.

Against the backdrop of His teaching on relationships, Jesus emphasized the impact of reconciliation on our spiritual lives. He offered clear direction to those who have offended others:

> Therefore if you are presenting your offering at the altar, and there remember that your brother has something against you, leave your offering there before the altar and go; first be reconciled to your brother, and then come and present your offering. (Matt. 5:23–24)

What a concept! Nowhere else in Scripture are we told to stop praying or desist from worshiping God in order to handle our personal business. But Jesus reminds us that our relationships with others affect our relationship with our Father. We cannot ascend the vertical ladder to God until the rope-bridge to our fellow man has been repaired and successfully crossed.

Leon Morris notes, "The interruption of so solemn an act emphasizes the overriding importance of reconciliation."[4] If we press on with our conversation with God without first seeking forgiveness, we need to realize that His ears are closed until we make that a priority. D. A. Carson eloquently points out, "Forget the worship service and be reconciled to your brother; and only then worship God. Men love to substitute ceremony for integrity, purity and love; but Jesus will have none of it."[5]

Jesus' illustration offers us two principles regarding reconciliation. First, *God is honored by immediate obedience.* Jesus' use of the Greek word for "first" in verse 24 denotes the priority: Now! Don't wait. Don't try to rationalize or find an excuse. Jesus demanded action!

The word for "reconcile" used here is found only once in the entire New Testament. It comes from the word meaning "to alter or change" or "to exchange,"[6] in the sense of "seeing to it that the angry brother, who neither seeks nor envisages reconciliation (v. 23), renounces his enmity."[7] Like a defendant before a judge, we approach those we have offended and plead guilty. We admit that the fault lies squarely on our shoulders. We come with humble and contrite hearts in order that the other person's enmity may cease and reconciliation may occur.

A second principle arises from these verses; *others are healed by vulnerable confessions.* Though we cannot control the offended person's response, we can offer a salve to help heal the wounds of those whom we have hurt. Our vulnerability paves the way towards reconciliation.

4. Leon Morris, *The Gospel according to Matthew* (Grand Rapids, Mich.: Eerdmans Publishing Co., 1992), p. 116.

5. D. A. Carson, *The Sermon on the Mount: An Evangelical Exposition of Matthew 5–7* (Grand Rapids, Mich.: Baker Book House, 1978), p. 42.

6. Gerhard Kittel, Geoffrey William Bromiley and Gerhard Friedrich, eds., *Theological Dictionary of the New Testament* (Grand Rapids, Mich.: Eerdmans Publishing Co., 1964), accessed through the Logos Library System.

7. Kittel, Bromiley and Friedrich, eds., *Theological Dictionary of the New Testament*, p. 253, accessed through the Logos Library System.

Offering Forgiveness

Now let's look at the other side of the chasm. What does Scripture say regarding the nature of forgiveness?

> Then Peter came and said to Him, "Lord, how often shall my brother sin against me and I forgive him? Up to seven times?" (Matt. 18:21)

Notice how Peter acts the part of the teacher's pet. Not only does he ask the question, but then he attempts to reveal the answer before Jesus has an opportunity to respond. In addition, Peter's attitude of self-righteousness is revealed in his answer. The rabbis in that day deduced from the first chapter of Amos that forgiveness could only be extended three times.[8] They believed that each person got three strikes, and after that, they were out! So Peter doubled the "acceptable quota" of forgiveness and added one for good measure.

But Jesus goes even further. His idea of forgiveness is clear in His response to Peter's question:

> Jesus said to him, "I do not say to you, up to seven times, but up to seventy times seven." (v. 22)

Commentator William Barclay notes, "Peter expected to be warmly commended; but Jesus's [sic] answer was that the Christian must forgive seventy times seven. In other words there is no reckonable limit to forgiveness."[9]

How about us? At what point does a debt become too great to be forgiven? Personalize the question by picturing yourself coming before Jesus with a real-life situation. Maybe your boss continually demeans you at work. Maybe your children are rebellious and ungrateful. Maybe your parents have never uttered words of affirmation. Perhaps you have a spouse who treats you poorly. What would Jesus tell you to do in these situations? Seventy times seven means you forgive so often that you don't remember the first time you forgave. And it also means that you leave behind the baggage of earlier offenses.

As Peter's jaw dropped and the other disciples were busy trying to multiply seventy times seven, Jesus punctuated his point with a

---

8. William Barclay, *The Gospel of Matthew*, Vol. 2 (*Chapters 11–28*), rev. ed (Philadelphia, Penn.: Westminster Press, 1975), p. 193.

9. Barclay, *The Gospel of Matthew*, p. 193.

parable about an unforgiving slave and a gracious king. In the story, a king attempts to settle a few accounts with his slaves. One slave owed a sum of ten thousand talents (Matt. 18:24), an astronomical amount in that day. How much was a talent worth? About six thousand days' wages for the average laborer. Today that might be equivalent to $10 million. It would take this slave roughly sixty million days to work off his debt![10] Recognizing the inability of this slave to pay his debt, the king commanded him and his family to be sold into slavery (Matt. 18:25). What was the slave's immediate response?

> "So the slave fell to the ground and prostrated himself before him, saying, 'Have patience with me and I will repay you everything.'" (v. 26)

The king's heart softened. Instead of waiting for his slave to repay him, he did an unusual thing:

> "And the lord of that slave felt compassion and released him and forgave him the debt." (v. 27)

What a picture of our salvation! Christ died to release us from a debt of sin we could never pay back. The Greek word for "release" in verse 27 carries the same meaning as the word "forgiveness" that Peter used in verse 21. We release the right to "get even" for the pain inflicted upon us. Archibald Hart described the act of forgiveness as "surrendering my right to hurt you for hurting me."[11]

The gracious lord gave up his right to inflict punishment upon the slave. Instead, he mercifully forgave his slave's enormous debt. But, amazingly, this slave quickly forgot the example of grace exhibited to him.

> "But that slave went out and found one of his fellow slaves who owed him a hundred denarii; and he seized him and began to choke him, saying, 'Pay back what you owe.' So his fellow slave fell to the ground and began to plead with him, saying, 'Have patience with me and I will repay you.' But he was unwilling and went and threw him in prison until he should pay back what was owed." (Matt. 18:28–30)

10. Craig S. Keener, *The IVP Bible Background Commentary: New Testament* (Downers Grove, Ill.: InterVarsity Press, 1993), p. 95.

11. Archibald Hart, as quoted by Charles R. Swindoll in *The Tale of the Tardy Oxcart and 1,502 Other Stories* (Nashville, Tenn.: Word Publishing, 1998), p. 216.

Look at the disparity of debts owed by the two slaves: a hundred denarii versus ten thousand talents! A denarius represented one day's wages for a common worker, or about sixteen cents.[12] The first slave, released from a $10 million debt, refused to let $16 slide! While his debt was impossible to pay back, the slave who owed a hundred denarii could have paid off his debt in less than four months.

Notice the different reactions of the king and the slave. The king responded with compassion; his slave responded with hurtful actions and an unforgiving heart. The lord set his slave free, but the slave put another man in shackles.

How did the king respond when he got word of his slave's actions? Once the king heard of the hypocrisy, he exchanged mercy for justice:

> "Then summoning him, his lord said to him, 'You wicked slave, I forgave you all that debt because you pleaded with me. Should you not also have had mercy on your fellow slave, in the same way that I had mercy on you?' And his lord, moved with anger, handed him over to the torturers until he should repay all that was owed him." (Matt.18:32–34)

The king's sentiment brings to mind a verse from the book of Luke: "From everyone who has been given much, much will be required" (12:48). Much had been given to the king's slave, and much was required of him. But he failed the test, so his master had the debt taken out of his flesh through torture, a relatively common practice in the ancient Near East.[13]

Thankfully, Jesus' teaching did not end with this servant's horrible demise. Instead, He connected this parable to our lives.

> "My heavenly Father will also do the same to you, if each of you does not forgive his brother from your heart." (Matt.18:35)

You mean God will punish His servants for failing to forgive others? That's what the Bible says! God states that He disciplines

12. John F. Walvoord, *The Bible Knowledge Commentary: An Exposition of the Scriptures* (Wheaton, Ill.: Victor Books, 1985), vol. 2, p. 63, accessed through the Logos Library System.

13. Kittel, Bromiley and Friedrich, eds., *Theological Dictionary of the Old Testament*, p. 561–562, accessed through the Logos Library System.

those He loves (Heb. 12:6). William Ward acutely points out, "We are most like beasts when we kill. We are most like men when we judge. We are most like God when we forgive."[14] The adverse would also be true: "We are most unlike God when we don't forgive." When we stubbornly refuse to forgive other people, we trample the grace lavished on us.

Living It Out

Many of us have experienced being "handed over to the torturers" (Matt. 18:34). A friend betrays our trust, so we trade grace for grudges. A spouse cheats with our best friend, so we bypass compassion to take up the chains of bitterness. A parent abuses us in hurtful ways, so we banish reconciliation to the abyss of anger and unforgiveness. But Jesus reminds us that when we don't release from their debts those seeking forgiveness, we incur the very punishment we seek to inflict.

Two principles shine brightly from Jesus' parable. First, *to refuse to forgive anyone anything is hypocritical.* We ourselves have been forgiven *every transgression* at the Cross. There the maximum forgiveness was offered on our behalf. So we're called to offer the same forgiveness and reconciliation to others.

Secondly, *to refuse forgiveness inflicts inner torment on the offended.* If we persist in "ungrace" toward anyone—whether they ask for forgiveness or not—we avail ourselves to the "torturers," otherwise known as bitterness, hatred, anger, and malice.

We've all wronged others, and we've been wronged—some of us terribly. But either way, it's our move. God desires true, deep communion with His children. But until we reconcile our relationships with others, we pursue the Lord in vain. We can't achieve a brighter future until we seek reconciliation for hurts that have occurred in the past. So take the first step onto the fragile rope-bridge of forgiveness today. You won't regret it!

---

14. William Ward, as quoted by Charles R. Swindoll in *The Tale of the Tardy Oxcart and 1,502 Other Stories* (Nashville, Tenn.: Word Publishing, 1998), p. 216.

✸ Living Insights

What about those who don't seek forgiveness from us? What about the hurtful parent who died without ever saying, "I'm sorry. Please forgive me"? What about the disloyal friend who wounded you and then turned her back? What about the unfaithful husband or wife who left a gaping hole in your life? It's one thing when someone approaches us with a penitent heart. But what about those who never see or recognize their sin? Should we offer forgiveness when no one is asking for it?

Take a moment to read Matthew 18:15–17. According to this passage, how are we to respond to a believer who has hurt us?

_____

_____

_____

_____

According to verse 17, how should the church treat a believer who refuses to repent after being approached about his or her wrongful actions?

_____

_____

The question remains . . . should we forgive believers who refuse to repent?

Let's answer this by reading Luke 23:33–38. How does Christ react to those who are crucifying Him?

_____

_____

Forgiveness is not the same as a pardon. When we forgive, we simply release the person from the pain they inflicted upon us. A

18

would normally follow as a result of their actions. You may forgive *and* pardon, but you may also forgive *without* pardoning. For instance, you may forgive the drunk driver who took the life of your friend in a car crash, but still support the lifetime prison sentence as the just penalty for the drunk driver's wrongdoing.

When we forgive, we release the right to get even, hold a grudge, or harbor bitterness against someone for his or her transgression. Aren't you glad that we don't have a God who gets even every time we wrong Him deliberately or indirectly? Thankfully, we serve a gracious God who forgives.

Resolution: Clean Up the Past

This study guide contains four main sections: *looking back, looking ahead, looking within,* and *looking around.* At the end of each section, we will resolve to make a commitment before the Lord. In these past two chapters, we looked back with the intention of cleaning out the trash accumulated through our neglect and our sin. And we learned how to deal with past transgressions. Remember: those who ignore the lessons of the past are destined to repeat them!

Take a few moments now to read *My Story* by Cynthia Swindoll, Chuck's wife and partner in ministry. This poignant, gripping testimony chronicles Cynthia's journey across the rope-bridge of forgiveness.

My Story

by Cynthia Swindoll

*B*efore I get into my story, I want to give you a few brush strokes of our lives as a context for relating some very meaningful experiences in my life. In the fall of 1959, after four years of marriage, Chuck entered Dallas Theological Seminary. Now, as every student knows, there is a whole course of study throughout your time in seminary that is not written up as a part of the curriculum, as the Lord strategically designs some of the things you need to learn about Him and about servanthood. So, two years into our studies at Dallas Seminary, we began to experience some very painful things.

First, we learned that my mom had breast cancer, and they gave her about three years to live. She was in her early forties and my very dearest, dearest friend. Today I miss her so very much. Then I lost a baby girl when I was five-and-a-half months pregnant. Following the loss, the physician gave me some Demerol for the pain that gave me the worst migraine I had ever had. They just kept giving me Demerol, enough to do surgery, but the pain became unbearable. (Fourteen years later, I would learn that Demerol triggers migraines in me, but back then, we were completely in the dark.)

They called in another physician, a young internist, who said that I was having this kind of head pain because I felt I had caused the death of our baby. This one consultation became a huge turning point in our lives.

A few months later, I was again pregnant. Six weeks into that pregnancy, we were in Houston visiting my folks for the Christmas holidays when we were in a terrible car accident. Our fifteen-month-old son, Curt's, jaw was broken and I began to hemorrhage, a problem I would have throughout the pregnancy, which resulted in my having to be in bed most of the time, lying flat on my back.

By then I was seeing a psychiatrist who, along with the original doctor, was telling me that the depression I was experiencing was the result of my feeling that I had caused the death of my second child and that I was now trying to abort this one.

To summarize their counsel, every word, every dream, every experience with another person as far back as I could remember became like twisted metal in the midst of a tornado, enveloped with definitions and meanings that had little resemblances to the realities I thought I knew. Emotionally, I spiraled downward into an abyss of depression. But, because this was in Dallas in 1963, we felt we had to keep my emotional struggles a secret. So we sought the counsel of those outside the church.

One counselor was an atheist. One was a believer whose approach in counseling was very Freudian, and he believed in strongly medicating his patients, which he did to me. Some years later, he himself would overdose. Also, some years later we would learn that Demerol and other medications have an adverse affect on my body.

The medications, along with the unwise counselors, had created the deep pit of depression. The psalmist describes this scene in Psalm 1 as "walking in the counsel of the wicked, standing in the path of the sinners, and sitting in the seat of scoffers." I had taken up the way of the transgressor. And even though I did "delight in the law of the Lord," I chose to become absorbed with the way of the wicked. I was encouraged to get very angry and to blame others for whatever it was that caused any measure of turmoil. Each person's words and actions were like feathers in the wind, like chaff, around which I would build caricatures with whom I would go to war: my dad, Chuck, Chuck's parents, people in the church, anyone.

The depression led to attempts at suicide. Once I was in a coma for three days from a drug overdose. This abyss lasted for five years, during which time Chuck was the associate pastor at Grace Bible Church. And for two years he pastored a church in New England, where I again sought counseling, still from the ungodly, and I was still encouraged to get angry and express those emotions.

When Chuck was called to Irving Bible Church in 1967, I made two decisions. It was a move. A new beginning. A new church. New friends. Five years of this stuff had not yielded any peace so I would not go to another ungodly counselor. And I would discontinue all medications for depression. I would take a whole new approach in order to get a handle on the depression.

We developed a very close friendship with a couple that encouraged me to read a book by William Glasser called *Reality Therapy*. This book basically said, "You're not irresponsible because you're sick, you're sick because you're irresponsible." Let me say that again. "You're not irresponsible because you're sick, you're sick because you're irresponsible." In other words, you need to learn to take full responsibility for your thoughts and for your actions. Don't blame anyone.

I began to think constantly about being responsible for every thought and for every action. Acting responsibly became the stair steps for my climb out of the pit. As Paul wrote in 2 Corinthians 10:5, I began

> destroying speculations and every lofty thing raised up against the knowledge of God, and . . . taking every thought captive to the obedience of Christ.

My friendship with this couple led to my becoming involved in a very interesting Bible study class for women in North Dallas led by a woman named Susan. Susan intensely wanted to know what the Bible had to say about our roles as wives and mothers. She developed a little test, and she encouraged us to take it, which I did. Later, privately, she told me that the test had revealed that I was very, very angry and very, very depressed. I knew that! By then I had been in the pit for seven long years.

We talked about Isaiah 58, which translated into today's language as the spiritual journal of the children of Israel during a time when they felt they were doing everything right. Yet they felt that God did not see them or listen to them, and He was not answering their petitions when they fasted. God then told them through Isaiah that their fasts were for their own desires, as revealed by the way they were living. They were mistreating their employees. They were contentious, and their lives were filled with strife. This sounded like my biography!

Then Isaiah, in this great fifty-eighth chapter, communicated the fast that God desired:

> "Is this not the fast which I choose,
> To loosen the bonds of wickedness,
> To undo the bands of the yoke,
> And to let the oppressed go free
> And break every yoke?" (v. 6)

Within that list were some statements that had a profound influence on me. God's fast was "to loosen the bonds of wickedness, to feed the poor, to take the homeless into their homes, to undo the bands of the yoke." And we talked a lot about how we "yoke" people, how we oppress them. And then the passage goes on to say at the end of verse 7 that we are not to "hide ourselves from our own flesh."

Susan shared her personal experiences with this chapter. It all hit me like a ton of bricks. Chuck and I were in the ministry, ministering to the masses, while, in the words of Isaiah, we were "pointing the finger and speaking wickedness" regarding our relatives. Isaiah later says that if we choose the fast the Lord has chosen,

"Then your light will break out like the dawn,
And your recovery will speedily spring forth;
And your righteousness will go before you . . .
And you will be called the repairer of the breach,
The restorer of the streets in which to dwell."
(vv. 8, 12b)

It was also during this time that Chuck prepared a study of Matthew 18 and we were awestruck with the whole concept of the Lord's "handing us over to the torturers" if we did not forgive our brothers from our hearts (v. 34). Did this pit of depression, did this abyss represent my having been turned over to the torturers? We believed it did.

Chuck and I talked about forgiveness and its application in our own lives. I thought about how I had re-created people during the therapy sessions, mostly our relatives, with character traits that often had little resemblance to the people they really were. Their words and actions were like feathers—Isaiah calls them, "like chaff in the wind"—around which I would create all kinds of caricatures. I had learned these methods from the therapist who tried to make me believe I had killed my baby, and I was applying them in my own relationships.

This is exactly what Satan has done since the Garden of Eden. (In fact, the devil's name, *diabolos* in Greek, literally means "the accuser.") Individuals, relatives, would say or do one thing, and I would give it a totally different meaning from anything he or she had had in mind. I'm totally convinced of that now. I came to understand that I had unrealistic expectations of what most of these relationships should be. So I blamed others for things they did not do that I thought they should have done. I had not taken ownership or accepted responsibility for my own actions. That was so very important.

Susan encouraged me to take out a stack of paper and record on every sheet a different name that represented someone with whom I had a conflict. I had to record what he or she had done to me that had brought pain and also everything I had ever done to hurt him or her. That was hard, because you often don't know what you have done that has hurt someone else. All you know is that you have an adversarial relationship, an uncomfortable feeling when you are around them. The filter for my thoughts was Philippians 4:8. Part of the verse reads,

> Finally, brethren, whatever is true, whatever is honorable, whatever is right, whatever is pure, . . . dwell on these things.

It was unacceptable for me to dwell on the characters I had created within my own mind. I had to think on those things that were true and honest. I was then encouraged to bring all of these lists to the foot of the cross and, in quietness before our Lord, see every situation from the perspective of the One who had died for all of these sins. Both mine and the ones committed against me. What an awesome, awesome place—a holy place! It changes your thinking regarding the whole dynamic of every relationship.

I then needed to prepare my speech for each person and then prepare to go to them to ask their forgiveness with no blame whatsoever for anything they had done. It would be just for the purpose of asking them to forgive me. And the ones with the longest list were to be approached first. This I did, and the first person was my dad.

Now, my dad had tried to kill my mom one evening by choking her to death and had only released his hands when she passed out. And she did not die. I had to forgive him of that. He had asked my mom for a divorce when she was dying of cancer. I had to forgive him of that. My dad had a terrible temper, and he had unmercifully beaten my sister and me when we were growing up. The horrors of his beating my sister would never leave my memory. I had to forgive him of that. But none of these things were even mentioned. They had all been left at the foot of the cross. This was not about him; it was about me and what I had done that was not right in our relationship.

My dad had been a wonderful provider and had given me common sense in the midst of hardships. He was diligent, a very hard worker. And he had learned to read and write after he and my mom married. He had many positive traits, and I needed to honor him for those and respect the good qualities of character he had passed on to me. His response was wonderful, and I told him I loved him.

Next was my mother-in-law. Mrs. Swindoll and I had never gotten along very well from the very beginning. (Some of you have had that experience!) By this point, Chuck and I had been married fifteen years, so this war had gone on for a long time and the converstation had been primarily reduced to yes and no. She had told us not to bring the children over to her home, as she was afraid they would break her hand-painted china which she had everywhere. She just did not like little kiddos. And rather than seeing this as an opportunity to teach my children how to behave when surrounded by glass, I took out the sword and blamed her for not wanting to have a relationship with our children.

Chuck's parents would invite only Chuck out for lunch, not me or the children. Every encounter was uncomfortable. So I had to really pray a lot for the right timing. I learned that not only should your heart be right, but sometimes other people's hearts have to be prepared to receive your words and your request for forgiveness. However, you are responsible to go no matter what their response may be. But you need to be prepared. This preparation went on for weeks.

One day, as I was preparing to teach a class on Friday evening with some seminary wives on how God is not finished with us yet, I got the idea of asking Chuck's mom if she would mind preparing a little unfinished oil painting of a shepherd with his sheep. She seemed delighted that I would ask her to do this.

Now, I had been praying that the Lord would make it very clear as to when I was to ask her forgiveness. But that Friday, when I opened the door to greet Mr. and Mrs. Swindoll as they were delivering the painting, I was totally amazed at how warm she was toward me. I thought as they entered the door, *Oh, my goodness! Oh, my goodness! This is it. This is the time. What is my speech? What is my speech? Oh my, this is it.*

They sat down on the sofa and, believe it or not, all four little ones were playing and being very good. That was a miracle! I thought, *Okay, okay.* My heart was pounding as I looked her straight in the eyes and told her how very sorry I was for not having loved her as I should have. For not having respected her as my husband's mom. For all the times I had taken issue with her for so many things, most of which she never even knew about. (Only Chuck knew.) And for not having honored her as the Scriptures say we should honor our parents. I then asked her to please forgive me, to which she replied she would. Then I told her that I loved her, and we embraced.

I cannot tell you the relief of these experiences. On Sunday, we sat in church together, and she told me how she had called all the relatives the day before and told them what I had done. I thought, *Oops, do I have a list for any of those relatives?* But I didn't, and we were all rejoicing at our new relationship. I'm reminded of Proverbs 23:15–16:

> My son, if your heart is wise,
> My own heart also will be glad;
> And my inmost being will rejoice
> When your lips speak what is right.

After the experiences with my dad and with my mother-in-law, I felt for the first time that I had been redeemed from the torture. With God's help in applying His Word, I had responsibly climbed out of the pit of depression, and I have not suffered from depression since.

Our rejoicing was sweet all weekend and carried over into Monday, Chuck's day off. Around the middle of the afternoon, Chuck's dad called him and asked if Chuck would come over to their apartment. He said, "I think your mom is gone. She told me she wasn't feeling well and thought she would just take a little nap. She's not waking up. There's no movement, and I think she is gone."

She was gone. Our weekend of rejoicing had represented the hors d'oeuvres for her banquet in heaven, dining with the Son of God. I had asked her forgiveness only three days before. That Friday evening had represented the last opportunity I would have had to do the most important thing I would ever do with her.

I have since come to realize that my foolishness for those fifteen to sixteen years, the years the locusts had eaten (see Joel 1–3), had totally devoured every opportunity I would ever have to learn from the one who had given birth to the person who would mean the most to me upon this earth, and now her death forever sealed shut those doors of opportunity.

Furthermore, she would never get to know my heart, my passion for the world, and my desire to share the liberating power that comes from applying God's truth to our life experiences. I know what it is like to be "handed over to the torturers." But more importantly, I have learned the unbelievable healing that comes when we forgive from our hearts—truly, truly forgive. That's what the Cross and the Resurrection are all about.

A powerful thing happens when we come to the foot of the cross—we gain a true and honest perspective of all of the events of our lives. We bring everything before Him who died for all of the sins of the entire world. There He enables us to sort out all the twisted metal, all the debris of our life experiences. There we leave all those things that have been done to us, and there we are empowered to seek forgiveness from those we have wronged. This process, these very acts of forgiveness, are the brush strokes on the canvases of our lives, portraying the grace and mercy of the One who bore all of our sins upon the cross.

This process is what brings healing. We are released from the torturers, freed from blaming, freed from unrealistic expectations, and freed from the caricatures we created upon the chaff in the wind. From my experiences, I encourage you to not let your paints dry out. Don't wait too long. It's this process that restores the years the locusts have eaten so that you can say with the psalmist, "The Lord will rejoice when my lips speak what is right" (see Prov. 23:15–16).

Chapter 3

LOOKING AHEAD:
FOCUSING ON PRIORITIES
WE PURSUE

Matthew 6:26–33; Romans 12:1–21

Two words—that's it. Once you utter these two simple, single-syllable words, your life changes radically. One moment, your priorities revolve around *you:* developing *your* spiritual life, pursuing *your* hobbies, buying *your* groceries, paying *your* rent. The next, you gaze adoringly into the eyes of your soon-to-be spouse, take a deep breath, and whisper the words "I do." And your life is forever changed.

Most young couples have no idea how much commitment their wedding-day "I do" will require. They may end up owning a house in Beverly Hills, or they may find themselves eating macaroni and cheese for dinner every night. They may run marathons together, or one partner may have to empty the other's bedpans. But the success of their marriage will hinge, for better or worse, on how well they strive to keep "I do" a priority.

When Jesus was asked about the number-one priority in life, His answer was crystal clear. He summed up in two words the key to living: "Seek first." That's it! When you strive to "seek first" the kingdom of God, your life will never be the same.

When we're standing at the altar saying "I do," we often don't foresee the tests our marriage will face down the road. In the same way, most of us don't recognize the full implications of "seek first" for our spiritual lives. We may find ourselves fellowshipping at a booming megachurch or suffering through a painful church split. Our teenagers may become faithful believers or disobedient, wayward prodigals. Our spouses may be loving or abusive. Yet the Lord promises that if we continue to trust Him, He will meet our needs. The success of our spiritual lives depends on how well we "seek first the kingdom of God and His righteousness."

Simple Command, Sufficient Promise

As we work on ordering our priorities, let's journey back to a mountain in Galilee. Surrounded by twelve of his closest friends,

28

Jesus shared His vision regarding life's greatest priority:

> "But seek first His kingdom and His righteousness, and all these things will be added to you." (Matt. 6:33)

Let's look at two aspects of this verse that are vital for priority-setting. First, Jesus exhorts us to "Seek first His kingdom and His righteousness." Second, He offers a magnificent promise: "and all these things will be added to you."

Seeking God first is our responsibility. We can't control many aspects of our lives, but we can choose to seek the Lord. The stock market may soar and dip like a roller coaster. Our jobs may flourish and then flounder. Our families might encourage us one day and infuriate us the next. Our spouses may treat us kindly sometimes and terribly at others. But through the highs and lows, we have a choice: to seek God's face daily.

The imperative *seek* in the present tense could be translated "consistently seek." We are to *consistently seek* God. That means we don't walk down the aisle, say "I do" to Him, and then run away and leave Him at the altar. Instead, we're to pursue God with all our hearts, with the fervent love of a bride for her groom. When we do so, God promises to reward us with "all these things."

What does He mean by that? Take a look at verse 33 again. It begins with the word *but*. Now look back at verses 31–32 to discover what Jesus was referring to:

> "Do not worry then, saying, 'What will we eat?' or 'What will we drink?' or 'What will we wear for clothing?'" "For the Gentiles eagerly seek *all these things*; for your heavenly Father knows that you need *all these things*." (v. 32, emphasis added)

From verse 32, we can glean two tidbits of information about "all these things." First, the "Gentiles" (here representing unbelievers in general) strive for them. Second, God knows that we need them. So "all these things" represents food, drink, and clothing—some of the basics necessary for our survival. God promises to provide for all our needs, just as He provides for the birds of the air (v. 26). And yet we often strive to obtain "all these things" ourselves.

We display our lack of faith by prioritizing the material over the spiritual and spending our time worrying about the things we need and want.

Most of us fall into one of two camps: those who worry about receiving the most basic provisions and those who concern themselves with getting the "perks." Those of us who are concerned about the basics struggle to keep *our worry from eclipsing our faith in God*. Jesus reminded us in verses 26 and 30 that the Father values us greatly and He will provide for all of our needs. We can't receive more from God until we trust Him to meet our most basic physical and spiritual needs.

In contrast with those who worry about the basics, many of us strive for the "perks." We struggle to keep *our comfort from eclipsing our passion for God*. We have plenty of clothes, but not the latest brand-name outfit. We have a beautiful home, but not a lake house. We have furniture, but not enough antiques. Our toughest decision of the day is choosing between a ribeye at our favorite steak house and filet mignon at the trendy French bistro down the street. We resemble the Laodiceans, who stated proudly: "I am rich, and have become wealthy, and have need of nothing" (Rev. 3:17). To those who live comfortably from day to day, Jesus says, "Seek the Father first, and you will gain the proper perspective on your life." Remember that the Lord, not you, has provided for your every need.

We all concern ourselves in some measure with seeking material possessions. The tangibles can easily consume all our energy, while God receives our leftover passion. But Jesus reverses this trend, exhorting us to spend our greatest passion on the Lord by seeking Him above *all* else.

The "Stuff" Doesn't Satisfy

Sometimes God uses traumatic situations to get our attention. A horrible car accident represented a major turning point in the life of Stephen King, one of the most prolific and popular authors of our time. Through a shattered windshield, new priorities came into focus for him:

> A couple of years ago I found out what "you can't take it with you" means. I found out while I was lying in a ditch at the side of a country road, covered with mud and blood and with the tibia of my right leg poking out the side of my jeans like the branch of a tree taken down in a thunderstorm. I had a MasterCard in my wallet, but when you're

lying in a ditch with broken glass in your hair, no one accepts MasterCard.

We all know that life is ephemeral, but on that particular day and in the months that followed, I got a painful but extremely valuable look at life's simple backstage truths. We come in naked and broke. We may be dressed when we go out, but we're just as broke. Warren Buffet? Going to go out broke. Bill Gates? Going out broke. Tom Hanks? Going out broke. Steve King? Broke. Not a crying dime.

All the money you earn, all the stocks you buy, all the mutual funds you trade—all of that is mostly smoke and mirrors. It's still going to be a quarter-past getting late whether you tell the time on a Timex or a Rolex. No matter how large your bank account, no matter how many credit cards you have, sooner or later things will begin to go wrong with the only three things you have that you can really call your own: your body, your spirit and your mind.

So I want you to consider making your life one long gift to others. And why not? All you have is on loan, anyway. All that lasts is what you pass on.[1]

Why does it take something as traumatic as a nearly fatal car crash to get our attention? Why do we wait until we hear the words *cancer, terminal illness,* or *complication* to figure out the true meaning of life? Why do we fail to appreciate our families until we lose someone we love? We must get our priorities straight *before* tragedy strikes. Stephen King realized in a ditch that the "stuff of life" wouldn't comfort him in his coffin. So what is it that truly matters?

A Living Sacrifice

Stephen King rearranged his priorities and vowed make his life "one long gift to others." While this goal is certainly commendable, we as Christians are called to do even more. In his letter to the Romans, the apostle Paul exhorted believers to make their lives one long gift to God:

Therefore I urge you, brethren, by the mercies of God,

1. Stephen King, "What You Pass On," *Family Circle*, Nov. 1, 2001, p. 156.

to present your bodies a living and holy sacrifice, acceptable to God, which is your spiritual service of worship. (Rom. 12:1)

Paul himself identified with the temptation of striving for material possessions, physical satisfaction, and recognition, rather than seeking God (Rom. 7:14–25). Always practical, Paul described a way we can "seek God first" by offering ourselves to Him.

A Living Sacrifice

Harkening back to the language and images of the Old Testament, Paul urged us to offer ourselves as "living sacrifices." In the Old Testament, in order for a sacrifice to be acceptable to God, it had to meet three standards: it had to be the *best*; it needed to be *unblemished*; and it was meant to be offered *willingly*.

For our lives to be the *best* for God, whether at work, home, or in church, we must offer our greatest energy, thoughts, and actions as acts of worship. If the Lord becomes an afterthought or receives only our leftover passion, then we offer our life as a *lame lamb*.

For our lives to be *unblemished*, we must sensitize ourselves to sin and consistently seek forgiveness (1 John 1:9). If we come before God with impure motives, hidden sins, or unreconciled relationships, we offer our life as a *tainted lamb*.

For our lives to be offered *willingly*, we must approach the altar with all of our heart, mind, and strength. But the problem with a living sacrifice is that it keeps wanting to crawl off the altar![2] If we begrudgingly come before the Lord or offer service to please man rather than God, then we offer our life as a *reluctant lamb*.

Be Transformed, Not Conformed

If you struggle with being lame, tainted, or reluctant, join the crowd! Only Jesus offered his life as the perfect Lamb. But Paul's words remind us how our sacrifice can be pleasing to God:

And do not be conformed to this world, but be transformed by the renewing of your mind, so that you may prove what the will of God is, that which is good and acceptable and perfect. (Rom. 12:2)

2. Author unknown.

Eugene Peterson rendered the first part of this verse as:

> Don't become so well-adjusted to your culture that
> you fit into it without even thinking. (Rom. 12:2,
> THE MESSAGE)[3]

When our way of thinking mirrors the world's, we're *conformed*. But, in contrast, God calls us as Christians to be *transformed*. A person with a transformed life may drive the same car, live in the same house, and wear the same clothes as he or she did before, but that person will demonstrate radically different priorities. The world grasps for satisfaction from many sources, but Christians satisfy themselves with the Lord.

For a resolution to succeed, its progress must be measurable. For instance, when you resolve to lose weight, the scales will be brutally honest as to your progress. When we resolve to "seek God" as our first priority, we need some scales to measure our progress. In Romans 12:9–21 Paul provided seven marks of a living sacrifice. Place a bookmark in your Bible to mark this passage. Every few weeks, come back to these verses and see how far you've come!

Seven Marks of a Living Sacrifice

Most great painters set up their easels near a source of inspiration. Before they begin to paint, they have a vision for what they want to create. In the same way, we must learn to visualize what a living sacrifice looks like in order to become one. Paul painted a revealing picture of how a transformed believer lives, offering seven characteristics that we can model in our lives.

Love

> Let love be without hypocrisy. Abhor what is evil;
> cling to what is good. Be devoted to one another in
> brotherly love; give preference to one another in
> honor. (Rom. 12:9–10)

The word *love* runs like a wild stallion through the English language, galloping in and out of our sentences with unbridled freedom. Our kids "love" ice cream, our friends "love" the Yankees,

3. Eugene H. Peterson, *The Message: The New Testament, Psalms and Proverbs* (Colorado Springs, Colo.: NavPress Publishing Group, 1995), p. 331.

and we "love" our spouses. But Paul doesn't use the word *love* loosely. He corrals true love with four distinct fences:

- Love must be authentic—"Without hypocrisy."[4]
- Love must be discerning—"Abhor what is evil."
- Love must be affectionate—"Be devoted to one another in brotherly love."[5]
- Love must be honoring—"Give preference to one another in honor."

If we seek to offer our lives as living sacrifices to God, people will notice. They'll see that our love is without disguise, tough on sin, passionate for all people, and honoring to others.

Enthusiasm

> . . . not lagging behind in diligence, fervent in spirit. (Rom. 12:11)

The word *fervent* in this verse connotes "boiling, bubbling,"[6] like water fighting to get out of the pot when the heat reaches 212 degrees Fahrenheit. As Christ ignites our passion, we should approach all our endeavors with ardent enthusiasm—bubbling over with excitement and passionate about sharing the Gospel with others. Without enthusiasm, our churches, our families, and even our sacrificial lives will languish in the tepid water of mediocrity.

Patience

> . . . rejoicing in hope, persevering in tribulation, devoted to prayer . . . (Rom. 12:12)

In the Greek, this verse literally reads, "In hope, rejoicing; in tribulation, persevering; in prayer, devoted." Paul balanced his enthusiasm with patience. His enthusiasm took him on multiple mission trips across countless countries, but his patience helped him to endure the pain and loneliness of numerous trials and incarcerations.

---

4. The word meant *sincere, unfeigned,* or *undisguised.* James Strong, *Enhanced Strong's Lexicon* (Ontario, Canada: Woodside Bible Fellowship, 1996), accessed through the Logos Library System.

5. "Brotherly love" comes from the Greek word *philadelphia.*

6. Strong, *Enhanced Strong's Lexicon,* accessed through the Logos Library System.

Following Paul's example, we can cling to hope in the midst of tribulations by rejoicing in our future deliverance. When afflictions break our backs, we can endure. In every need, we can persevere with prayer. Remember that Jesus promised that this life would be filled with struggle (John 16:33). "Seeking God first" does not come without a price, but it's worth it!

Generosity

> . . . contributing to the needs of the saints . . .
> (Rom. 12:13a)

Part of sacrificial living involves giving to those in need. How's your giving? Look carefully over your check register. Of course, God expects all of us to graciously give to Him from our "first fruits," but we're also called to give above and beyond that to help others in need. And remember, we aren't limited to offering only financial help. All of us have opportunities to give our time, our energy, our resources, and our skills to meet needs in our families, churches, and communities.

Hospitality

> . . . practicing hospitality. (Rom. 12:13b)

Our vibrant relationship with Christ should be characterized by open hearts, open hands, and open doors. The word *hospitality* in Greek means "love to strangers."[7] How well do you show love to strangers? It's easy to invite your best friends over for dinner, but when was the last time you opened up your home to a homeless person? Or invited that struggling single mother and her kids to lunch? Or had your reclusive neighbors over for a barbecue? Be aware of open doors, and take the initiative to walk through them with faith!

Sympathy

> Rejoice with those who rejoice, and weep with those
> who weep. (Rom. 12:15)

Some Christians have a better track record with the former than with the latter. It can be easier to celebrate a victory with a joyful friend than to reach out to a suffering or wayward member

---

7. Strong, *Enhanced Strong's Lexicon*, accessed through the Logos Library System.

of our church. It often takes less effort to applaud from the sidelines than it does to truly sympathize with our brothers and sisters in their grief. But part of "seeking Him first" is giving of ourselves to support those in need.

On the other hand, we sometimes find it easier to weep at others' hurts and commiserate over their failures than to applaud their successes. Envy, hurt feelings, and a lack of self-confidence can make us bitter when we see others receive praise. Some of us feel more useful when helping out a weaker brother or sister than we do congratulating an extremely blessed or successful friend. But we're called to do both. As members of the body of Christ, we're to rejoice with those who are happy and weep alongside those who are hurting.

Humility

> . . . do not be haughty in mind, but associate with the lowly. Do not be wise in your own estimation. (Rom. 12:16b)

Paul's exhortations become more difficult to follow the further we go down the list! Theologian John Stott reminds us of Jesus' ministry to all kinds of people:

> Few kinds of pride are worse than snobbery. Snobs are obsessed with questions of status, with the stratification of society into 'upper' and 'lower' classes, or its division into distinctions of tribe and caste, and so with the company they keep. They forget that Jesus fraternized freely and naturally with social rejects, and calls his followers to do the same with equal freedom and naturalness.[8]

A living sacrifice knows no status—only service to the Lord, who receives its worship.

Greatheartedness

> Bless those who persecute you; bless and do not curse . . . Never pay back evil for evil to anyone . . . "But if your enemy is hungry, feed him, and if

---

8. John R. W. Stott, *Romans: Good News for the World* (Downers Grove, Ill.: InterVarsity Press, 1994), p. 333.

he is thirsty, give him a drink; for in so doing you will heap burning coals on his head." (Rom. 12:14, 17a, 20)

It's a made-up word, but the term *greatheartedness* fits with our final mark of a living sacrifice! Greatheartedness may be the most difficult characteristic of a living sacrifice. It defies our thirst for revenge and justice. But those who keep God as their first priority respond to blatant evil with bountiful good. When God sought to repair the chasm between depraved human beings and Himself, He overcame our evil with perfect love in the form of a perfect sacrifice—His Son, Jesus Christ. While the world strives for payback, getting even, and holding grudges, believers should respond with charity, compassion, and courage to trust God with the results.

As you look ahead to the coming year, realize that every decision you make will reflect your priorities. Pursue God's will for your life first by offering up your life as a living sacrifice. Resolve that in the next few months, your life will be marked by love, enthusiasm, patience, generosity, hospitality, humility, and greatheartedness. And remember, above all, to seek God first! He promises that when you do, all kinds of blessings "will be added to you."

 Living Insights

The third verse of the hymn "Be Thou My Vision" captures the struggle between striving for God and striving for material blessings.

> Riches I heed not, nor man's empty praise,
> Thou mine inheritance, now and always:
> Thou and Thou only, first in my heart,
> High King of heaven, my Treasure Thou art.[9]

"Riches" and "empty praise" represent our desire for material blessings. Write down the material things you've been striving to acquire.

_____

_____

9. Mary Byrne, trans., "Be Thou My Vision," *Hymns for the Family of God* (Nashville, Tenn.: Paragon Associates Inc, 1976), p. 468.

How has the pursuit of these things affected your relationship with God?

_____

_____

_____

_____

Think about the seven marks of a living sacrifice. In what ways does your life exhibit love, enthusiasm, patience, generosity, hospitality, sympathy, humility, and greatheartedness? What areas could use improvement?

_____

_____

_____

_____

What steps can you take to re-order your spiritual priorities? What changes do you need to make in your life in order to truly "seek God first"?

_____

_____

_____

_____

Now write out a prayer to God, leaving the "wants" behind and putting yourself on the altar as a living sacrifice. List some ways that you will offer your life up to God more completely.

_____

_____

_____

_____

_____

_____

_____

_____

_____

_____

_____

_____

_____

Chapter 4

LOOKING WITHIN: DISCOVERING THE ESSENTIALS OF THE CHURCH

Matthew 16:13–18; Acts 2:41–47

Many people regard church attendance as a "speed bump" on the highway of life. One aspect of the service may touch their hearts for a moment, but the memories of the songs, the message, and the people quickly subside into nothingness as they continue on with their daily routines.

In her early years, Pulitzer Prize-winning writer Annie Dillard found church a hindrance to true worship rather than a help. She describes her church experience this way:

> Week after week I was moved by the pitiableness of the bare linoleum-floored sacristy which no flowers could cheer or soften, by the terrible singing I so loved, by the fatigued Bible readings, the lagging emptiness and dilution of the liturgy, the horrifying vacuity of the sermon, and by the fog of dreary senselessness pervading the whole, which existed alongside, and probably caused, the wonder of the fact that we came; we returned; we showed up; week after week, we went through with it.[1]

Is church a drudge or a delight for you? Unfortunately, many of us find it a drudge. Why? Often, it's because we have replaced the purposes of the church with the programs of the church. As a result, we feel only the small "speed bump" on Sunday morning. We've forgotten that the church began as a mighty volcano, overflowing with the power of God and spilling passion into the hearts of people.

This chapter was adapted from chapters 2–3 in the Bible study guide The Bride: Renewing Our Passion for the Church, written by Gary Matlack, from the Bible teaching ministry of Charles R. Swindoll (Anaheim, Calif.: Insight for Living, 1994).

1. Annie Dillard, as quoted by Philip Yancey in Church: Why Bother? (Grand Rapids, Mich.: Zondervan Publishing, 1998), p. 22.

In this chapter, we'll visit a pagan city to hear an incredible prophecy about the church. Then we'll rediscover the power that flowed when the Holy Spirit was poured out at Pentecost. And lastly, we'll walk together through Acts 2 to discover God's passion and purposes for His church, the bride of Christ.

Setting the Scene

Upon Herod's death in 4 B.C., the city of Caesarea came under the authority of Philip the Tetrarch. Philip added the word *Philippi* to the city's name to distinguish it from the coastal city of Caesarea.[2] It was here in Caesarea Philippi, a largely Gentile city, that Jesus revealed a curious and wonderful prophecy about Himself and the church.

Walking in the midst of this diverse pagan community, Jesus turned to his disciples and asked, "Who do people say that the Son of Man is?" (Matt. 16:13). Then Jesus probed more deeply by asking, "But who do *you* say that I am?" (v. 15, emphasis added). It was one thing for the disciples to relay the thoughts of the crowd. But Jesus knew that it would be quite another for one of the disciples to step up with the right answer to this vital question!

In the text, you will notice three words that usually spell disaster: "Simon Peter answered . . ." Peter's foot often had a tendency to find its way into his mouth. But not this time! The gospel of Matthew climaxes with Peter's brilliant answer to the greatest question of all. In the fertile hills of Mt. Hermon, away from the multitudes, he solved the riddle, announcing:

> "You are the Christ, the Son of the living God."
> (Matt. 16:16)

Prophecy about the Church

Jesus affirmed Peter for his wise answer. Then He prophesied about Peter's role in the birth and growth of a new institution called *the church*:

> "I also say to you that you are Peter, and upon this rock I will build My church; and the gates of Hades will not overpower it." (Matt. 16:18)

---

2. J. D. Douglas, *New Bible Dictionary* (Wheaton, Ill.: Tyndale House, 1996), accessed through the Logos Library System.

From this verse, we can glean some key prophecies about the church:

> **"I"**—Christ builds the church, not pastors, people, or programs.
>
> **"will"** This verb appears in the future tense. At the time that Christ was speaking, the church had not yet been established.
>
> **"build"**—The growth of the church is a process, not a completed act.
>
> **"My"**—Christ, not the clergy, elders, or members, is the owner of the church.
>
> **"church"**—In Greek, the word *ekklesia* connotes people "called out from their homes into . . . an assembly"[3] and gathered for a distinct purpose.
>
> **"the gates of Hades will not overpower it"**—Neither Satan and his forces nor anything else on earth can destroy the church that Christ has established.

As we'll soon see, at Pentecost this incredible prophecy regarding the church became a reality.

Purposes of the Church

The book is Acts, chapter 2. The setting is Jerusalem. The event? The birth of the church. The Holy Spirit descends, and the Gospel blows through the city like a fresh ocean breeze. Simon Peter preaches the sermon of his life, which God uses like a fisherman's net to pull three thousand souls into His kingdom. Acts 2:42–45 tells what happens next:

> They were continually devoting themselves to the apostles' teaching and to fellowship, to the breaking of bread and to prayer.
> Everyone kept feeling a sense of awe; and many wonders and signs were taking place through the apostles. And all those who had believed were

---

3. James Strong, *Enhanced Strong's Lexicon* (Ontario: Woodside Bible Fellowship, 1996), accessed through the Logos Library System.

together and had all things in common; and they
began selling their property and possessions and were
sharing them with all, as anyone might have need.

Imagine that! A thriving community of new believers with no
pastor, no bylaws, no high-powered programs, and an incomplete
Bible. Yet they still managed to fulfill the primary purpose of the
church—glorifying God.

Day by day continuing with one mind in the temple,
and breaking bread from house to house, they were
taking their meals together with gladness and sincerity of heart, praising God and having favor with
all the people. And the Lord was adding to their
number day by day those who were being saved.
(vv. 46–47)

How did these early believers achieve such close fellowship?
They had objectives to follow, a path to run on that took them
straight to the glory of God. And so do we!

In this passage, we find four major objectives that are important
for every Christ-centered, Bible-believing church to pursue, regardless of size, style, culture, or denomination. Together, these objectives comprise the acronym **WIFE**, which is appropriate for Christ's
bride, don't you think?

Worship

Instruction

Fellowship

Evangelism

Worship and instruction are primarily vertical activities, between us and God. Fellowship and evangelism deal primarily with
our horizontal relationships with others, both within and outside
the body of Christ.

W Is for Worship

Like an irresistible perfume, worship's holy fragrance wafted
from this fledgling community. The Greek term for "continually
devoting" (Acts 1:14; 2:42) suggests a constant, steadfast persis-
tence. This was no halfhearted group of pew warmers! When these
early saints gathered, their prayers overflowed with praise. Their

meetings radiated with intense devotion. As they sat under the apostles' teaching, assembled for fellowship and prayer, and took their meals together, they kept their focus on the Lord God.

The immediate result of the people's devotion was a "sense of awe" (2:43a). The Greek literally reads, "And came to every soul fear." This holy fear was more than music-induced goose bumps or "warm fuzzies" from a sermon. As the people worshiped, they were overcome with the magnificence of God's holiness.

It's clear that these people did not sit in rigid, cold formality, unable to release emotion. Acts 2:46 tells us, "day by day continuing with one mind in the temple, and breaking bread from house to house, they were taking their meals together with gladness and sincerity of heart" (literally, "simplicity of heart"), which erupted in praise to God (v. 47). This description illustrates what worship is: a human response to divine revelation. And when true worship occurs, God is pleased, for He seeks genuine worshipers (John 4:23).

The early church effervesced with the spontaneous expression of heartfelt worship. But unfortunately, many of today's churches have replaced that genuine worship with dull, dry religious meetings. Ask yourself if your church experience fits this description:

> In many (most?) churches there are programs and activities . . . but so little worship. There are songs and anthems and musicals . . . but so little worship. There are announcements and readings and prayers . . . but so little worship. The meetings are regular, but dull and predictable. The events are held on time, led by well-meaning people, supported by folks who are faithful and dedicated . . . but that tip-toe expectancy and awe-inspiring delight mixed with a mysterious sense of the fear of almighty God are missing. [4]

The church, as the bride of Christ, must see all she does through the lens of true worship.

I Is for Instruction

A closer look at Acts 2 reveals that the early Christians not only worshiped God, they also learned His Word. Once again, observe

4. Charles R. Swindoll, *The Bride: Renewing Our Passion for the Church* (Grand Rapids, Mich.: Zondervan Publishing House, 1994), p. 40 (page citation is to the second printing).

verse 42: "They were continually devoting themselves to the apostles' teaching." This implies that God's Word as taught by the apostles was embraced by the early church. Note that instruction is listed first in the order of activities. Why? Because babies need food. Remember, these brand-new believers had just tasted the milk of the Gospel. Now they required the meat of the Word for growth.

The apostles considered the ministry of God's Word so important that they delegated other duties in order to ensure unobstructed teaching (see Acts 6:1–6). They refused to allow the pressing demands of the ministry, as important as they were, to keep them from their primary task of feeding the flock with God's truth.

The ministry of the Word is no less important today. We rejoice over the lost sheep that hear the Gospel and establish a relationship with Christ. But if these sheep don't become a part of the church body, receiving spiritual meat through solid teaching week after week, they will become sickly and scrawny! Starving sheep lack spiritual strength for daily living, and their lack of knowledge makes them easy prey for false teaching. It is essential that we, as sheep, hunger after the truth and instruction that come from studying God's Word.

F Is for Fellowship

The early Christians would find it difficult to relate to our custom of sneaking into the back pew at church, sitting there inconspicuously through the service, and then slipping out the back door during the closing prayer. They gathered not only to worship and learn, but to engage in intimate friendships with one another. They celebrated and mourned, laughed and cried, cared for and sacrificed for one another. They came for *real fellowship*—one of the activities to which they continually devoted themselves (Acts 2:42).

The Greek word for fellowship, *koinonia*, signifies a close relationship. Its root, *koinos*, means "common" or "communal."[5] The early church was a close, sharing group. That's the idea of verse 44:

> And all those who had believed were together and
> had all things in common.

5. Walter Bauer, *A Greek-English Lexicon of the New Testament and Other Early Christian Literature*, 2d ed. Revised and augmented by F. Wilbur Gingrich and Frederick W. Danker, from Walter Bauer's 5th ed., 1958 (Chicago, Ill.: University of Chicago Press, 1979), pp. 438–39.

Fellowship is genuine Christianity freely shared among God's family members. Isn't it sad to think of how many Christians today are missing this kind of closeness? Sermons and songs provide only part of a vital worship encounter. We need true fellowship with others, too. If we roll in and out of church each week, never getting involved, we are missing the point. If we aren't interacting with others, we really haven't tasted the sweet joy of fellowship.

Acts 2:45 portrays true fellowship as an act of sharing something tangible to meet a need:

> And they began selling their property and posses-
> sions and were sharing them with all, as anyone
> might have need.

What a picture of sacrificial giving! Believers were selling land and personal belongings and then channeling the proceeds to others in the church. They weren't seeking to purchase bigger and more elaborate homes. They weren't trying to gain greater wealth or stature in the community. They weren't striving for more land or livestock. They weren't buying fine clothing and jewelry. They gave up their own rights and desires in order to meet the needs of others.

Can you imagine what would happen if we did the same? If we gave to the needy in our congregation instead of buying a new car? If we offered to pay for someone else's education instead of buying the latest stock? If we went on a mission trip instead of taking a vacation? God wants us to be good stewards of our resources, but He also wants us to help build up those within the body who have particular needs. But many of us would rather let our funds grow in the vat of plenty than help feed the needy. That's not how the church was meant to be! Be on the lookout for needs in your church that you have the opportunity to meet.

E Is for Evangelism

The early church was caught in the flow of the Gospel of Christ. The love of God flooded from their hearts, and, as they expressed the reality of Christ to a watching world, the ranks of the converted swelled. The church reached out to others, actively modeling evangelism—our fourth and final objective for the church.

Acts 2:47b reads, "And the Lord was adding to their number day by day those who were being saved." Is it any wonder that God blessed the Jerusalem church with growth? Christians there offered love and acceptance. They modeled vulnerability, compassion, caring, and giving. They radiated winsomeness and joy. The aroma of these qualities drifted from the church into the nostrils of Jerusalem like the lovely smell of a Sunday pot roast. And the world came to dinner!

The early church set a powerful example for us to follow. They glorified God by keeping the four objectives of worship, instruction, fellowship, and evangelism. Keep in mind that a church may have *more* than these four pillars, but no faithful church will have *less*. The apostles built the early church upon these principles. If we don't follow their blueprint, our churches will crumble due to lethargy, malnourishment, selfishness, and fruitlessness. How can you help your church recapture the joy of worship, instruction, fellowship, and evangelism?

 Living Insights

Like stars to the early seafarers, principles guide us through the deep waters of life. When asked, most influential people can produce a list of meaningful principles for life as quickly as a sailor can tie a bowline. Former president Thomas Jefferson once stated, "In matters of style, swim with the current; in matters of principle, stand like a rock."[6]

When another former president, James Garfield, was a boy, an elderly man gave him a list of principles that guided him to the end of his days. Some bright stars from his list include:

Make few promises. . . .
Always speak the truth.
When you speak to a person look into his eyes.
Save when you are young to spend when you are old.
Never run into debt unless you see a way out
    again. . . .
Your character cannot be essentially injured except
    by your own acts.
If anybody speaks evil of you let your life be so that
    no one believes him.[7]

6. Thomas Jefferson, www.brainyquote.com/quotes/quotes/t/q121032.html, accessed on September 6, 2002.

7. Paul Lee Tan, *Encyclopedia of 7,700 Illustrations*, electronic ed. (Garland, Tex: Bible Communications, 1996), accessed through the Logos Library System.

Unfortunately, many of our church ministries are guided by methods rather than principles. We tend to cling to particular forms such as small groups, Sunday school, or a specific worship style. We often focus on these forms instead of the true functions of the church, which are worship, instruction, fellowship, and evangelism. Valuing a particular form over the function of the church is like busying ourselves with swabbing the decks rather than navigating our course. If every sailor has the wrong focus, our ship will eventually sink. But Warren and David Wiersbe steer us back on course with these ten principles of a healthy ministry:

Number one: the foundation of ministry is character.

Number two: the nature of ministry is service.

Number three: the motive for ministry is love.

Number four: the measure of ministry is sacrifice.

Number five: the authority of ministry is submission.

Number six: the purpose of ministry is the glory of God.

Number seven: the tools of ministry are prayer and the Word of God.

Number eight: the privilege of ministry is growth.

Number nine: the power of ministry is the Holy Spirit.

Number ten: the model for ministry is Jesus Christ.[8]

Think about your own ministry at your church. What personal ministries are you involved with? You may be in a small group. You may sing in the choir or teach a Bible study class. You may be involved with a greeting or hospitality ministry. You may volunteer to work in a soup kitchen or do some other volunteer ministry. Which of the principles listed do you need to bolster in your current ministry life?

_____

_____

8. These ten principles are taken from Warren W. Wiersbe and David Wiersbe, *Making Sense of the Ministry* (1983; reprint, Grand Rapids, Mich.: Baker Book House, 1989), p. 31–46.

_____

_____

Now think about these principles for a moment in the larger context of your church. How might your church incorporate these principles into its ministry programs? How can your church better glorify God? How can you use your current involvement in ministry to help those in your church live up to these ten principles?

_____

_____

_____

_____

Regardless of how well we harness the wind, batten down the hatches, or steer the rudder, if we set sail without principles, we drift aimlessly in a vast ocean. Keep God's Word and His principles in the forefront of your mind, and you'll stay on course!

Chapter 5

LOOKING WITHIN:
COMING TO TERMS WITH
OURSELVES

Romans 7:14–25

The 2001 movie *A Beautiful Mind* depicts the real-life battle of brilliant mathematician John Forbes Nash Jr. against mental illness. At the peak of his genius, with a promising career in his sights, Nash began to lose his grip on reality. Severe schizophrenia and delirium sent his life into a destructive downward spiral that jeopardized his career, his marriage, and his reputation in the field of mathematics.

Nash later described his struggle this way:

> "I started to . . . hear voices all the time. I began to hear something like telephone calls in my head, from people opposed to my ideas . . . The delirium was like a dream from which I seemed never to awake." [1]

His hard-fought battle lasted over thirty years, but Nash finally awoke. By the early 1990s, he had recovered remarkably from his mental illness, and in 1994, John Forbes Nash Jr. won the prestigious Nobel Prize in Economic Science for the impact of his work on economic theory.

The apostle Paul might have sympathized somewhat with Nash's struggle. The great apostle sought to rid himself of the evil thoughts and desires of his flesh, just as the great mathematician tried desperately to fend off the destructive messages his mind was sending. Yet Paul continued to struggle, as all Christians do, to live a righteous life while avoiding the pitfalls of sin.

Parts of this chapter have been adapted from "Clearing the Hurdle of Carnality," in the Bible study guide *Clearing the High Hurdles: Overcoming Obstacles to Obeying God's Call*, written by Bryce Klabunde, from the Bible-teaching ministry of Charles R. Swindoll (Anaheim, Calif.: Insight for Living, 1995), pp. 63–71.

1. John Forbes Nash Jr., at www-groups.dcs.st-and.ac.uk/~history/Mathematicians/Nash.html, accessed on July 15, 2002.

The Struggle against the Flesh

Paul sought to fulfill the worthy desires of the Spirit, yet he fought a constant battle against the desires of his flesh. He recorded his conflicting thoughts and emotions in Romans 7:14–15:

> For we know that the Law is spiritual, but I am of flesh, sold into bondage to sin. For what I am doing, I do not understand; for I am not practicing what I would like to do, but I am doing the very thing I hate.

Can you relate? Most of us know what it's like to do something that we wish we weren't doing. From our spiritual birth to our physical death, the Holy Spirit wages war against our own flesh— that powerful physical force that pursues its own ends apart from God. But the flesh can never be completely reformed. Our sinful nature remains, seeking its own desires.

We continue to grow in our faith. We mature spiritually, and we may even assume respected positions of leadership in the church. But our flesh never grows up! In fact, the more we mature, the greater our inner conflict grows. Wickedness is always lurking within us, ready to raise its powerful fist and take control.

Scripture describes an unregenerate person's thoughts as "only evil all the time" (Gen. 6:5; see also 8:21). The Lord stated that "the heart is deceitful above all things and beyond cure. Who can understand it?" (Jer. 17:9 NIV). Because we possess sinful natures and deceitful hearts, we must be born again through faith in Jesus Christ in order to receive eternal life. Paul wrote, "If anyone is in Christ, he is a new creation; the old has gone, the new has come!" (2 Cor. 5:17).[2]

Paul knew firsthand the tension between the old creation and the new. He went on to describe its complexities:

> But if I do the very thing I do not want to do, I agree with the Law, confessing that the Law is good. So now, no longer am I the one doing it, but sin which dwells in me. (Rom. 7:16–17)

---

2. John Witmer, "Heart," in *The Theological Wordbook*, ed. Charles R. Swindoll and Roy B. Zuck (Nashville, Tenn.: Word Publishing, 2000).

The term "Law" designates God's commands and principles as expressions of His will.[3] God's Law served a specific purpose—it pointed people towards Him. Since no one could keep the Law perfectly in its entirety, all of God's people would be forced to confront their sin. The apostle Paul's sinful nature was revealed by his inability to keep the Law and by the desires of his flesh to commit sin. But he realized that his battle wasn't just between the flesh and the Spirit—it was also a battle of the *heart*.

The Battle of the Heart

Think about your heart for a moment. It beats around 70 times per minute. That's 4,200 times an hour, 16,800 times a day, 691,600 times a week. Your heart may seem small, but it's powerful. And the consequences of not taking care of it can be deadly! You depend upon your heart to pump life-giving blood through your body. In the same way, the condition of your spiritual heart determines the state of your spiritual life.

Scripture uses the word *heart* more than eight hundred times, but rarely does this term refer to the literal physical organ of the human body. It almost always points to the spiritual heart— representing the mind as the center of knowledge, the soul as the seat of human emotions, and the spirit as that which responds to God. Our hearts are the parts within us that are eternal. They make us who we truly are.[4]

The apostle Paul felt the flesh and the Spirit playing tug-of-war for control of his heart. He described this "game" in the following way:

> For I know that nothing good dwells in me, that is, in my flesh; for the willing is present in me, but the doing of the good is not. For the good that I want, I do not do, but I practice the very evil that I do not want. But if I am doing the very thing I do not want, I am no longer the one doing it, but sin which dwells in me. (Rom. 7:18–20)

The Holy Spirit urged Paul to do good, but Paul's sinful nature often won out. Paul even said that he wasn't the one committing

---

3. J. D. Douglas, ed., *New Bible Dictionary*, 2d edition (Wheaton, Ill.: Tyndale House Publishers, Inc., 1987), see "Law."

4. Witmer, "Heart," in *The Theological Wordbook*.

the sins, but the sinful nature within him (v. 20). He recognized that the powerful pull of sin influenced him to do things that did not please God.

Paul went on to describe the difference between the law of God and the law of the sinful nature:

> I find then the principle that evil is present in me, the one who wants to do good. For I joyfully concur with the law of God in the inner man, but I see a different law in the members of my body, waging war against the law of my mind and making me a prisoner of the law of sin which is in my members. (vv. 21–23)

Paul "joyfully concurred with the law of God" (v. 22). He recognized that the Holy Spirit within him had true control over his heart. But he didn't deny that a different law waged war against his flesh, striking at his mind and emotions. The law of the flesh sought to imprison him, but the law of God sought to set him free.

When the world looks at Christians, they expect to see caring hearts, positive attitudes, kind words, and good deeds. When they see hard hearts, negative attitudes, unkind words, and sinful actions, they say, "I thought he was a Christian, but look what he did!" Or, "She's supposed to be a Christian, but did you hear what she just said?" When others look at you, knowing you're a Christian, they expect to see a changed heart and a transformed life.

Paul had been granted the treasure of new life in Christ, and he wanted his life to reflect the true source of that treasure. Though he continued to battle against sin as long as he lived on earth, his ministry poured out like a flood of riches upon the people of Asia Minor. The Gospel he preached there radically changed the lives of thousands. He started churches and ministered to people, serving selflessly even while experiencing severe persecution.

The full impact of Paul's example and teachings upon the church cannot be measured by human standards. He was a man who still struggled with sin like the rest of us. Yet he passionately pursued God with his *heart*, crying out to the Lord:

> Wretched man that I am! Who will set me free from the body of this death? Thanks be to God through Jesus Christ our Lord! So then, on the one hand I myself with my mind am serving the law of God,

but on the other, with my flesh the law of sin.
(Rom. 7:24–25)

Paul served the law of God over the law of sin. He expressed his thanksgiving to the Lord because he knew that the final victory over sin was his through the Holy Spirit:

> For the law of the Spirit of life in Christ Jesus has set you free from the law of sin and of death. . . . For the mind set on the flesh is death, but the mind set on the Spirit is life and peace. (vv. 8:2, 6)

The death and resurrection of Jesus Christ set Paul free from the law of sin and death. He rested in the peace of God, knowing that he had new life in the Spirit.

Three Types of People

As we mentioned earlier, the degree to which we allow the flesh or the Holy Spirit to control our hearts determines our spiritual condition. In the book of 1 Corinthians, Paul used this standard of measurement to identify three different types of people: the natural person, the spiritual person, and the carnal person.

The Natural Person

The unsaved person, completely controlled by the flesh, is called the "natural man." This person cannot and does not accept the things of the Spirit of God, because these things are spiritually discerned. The welcome mat of the natural person's heart is pulled in and the door bolted against spiritual truth. Paul describes this type of person in 1 Corinthians 2:14:

> But a natural man does not accept the things of the Spirit of God, for they are foolishness to him; and he cannot understand them, because they are spiritually appraised. (v. 14)

The Greek word for "foolishness" is *mōros,* from which we get the English word *moron.* A "foolish" person makes unwise or faulty moral judgments because he or she is unable to discern God's truth and purposes.[5] Spiritual matters seem foolish to the natural person

---

5. J. D. Douglas, ed., *New Bible Dictionary,* 2d edition (Wheaton, Ill.: Tyndale House Publishers, Inc., 1982), see "folly."

because he or she is ignorant of the truth. Just as the wondrous depths of the sea remain a mystery to us, the deep realities of life in God remain incomprehensible to the "natural man."

The Spiritual Person

In contrast, the "spiritual" person is controlled by the Holy Spirit. He or she grasps the truths of God's Word and is always hungry to hear more! Paul describes this kind of person in verses 15–16:

> But he who is spiritual appraises all things, yet he himself is appraised by no one. For who has known the mind of the Lord, that he will instruct Him? But we have the mind of Christ.

With the "mind of Christ," we can hear and experience the Spirit in new ways. As a result, subjects such as sin, grace, and forgiveness receive fresh meaning and power. The Spirit becomes our Teacher, Encourager, Comforter, and Guide. Yielding to His direction, we can glorify God with deeds of holiness—something that was impossible for us to do in our natural state.

Spiritual people will also realize that, unfortunately, their flesh did not pack up and leave once the Holy Spirit moved in! Our flesh despises this godly "Intruder" and determines to scratch and claw its way back into our lives. The spiritual person will be on guard constantly with the sword of the Spirit (the Word of God), ready to strike back against the desires of the flesh.

The Carnal Person

Paul goes on to describe the third category of person: the carnal, or "fleshly," believer. He writes:

> And I, brethren, could not speak to you as to spiritual men, but as to men of flesh, as to infants in Christ. I gave you milk to drink, not solid food; for you were not yet able to receive it. Indeed, even now you are not yet able, for you are still fleshly. For since there is jealousy and strife among you, are you not fleshly, and are you not walking like mere men? (1 Cor. 3:1–3)

The word *carnal* comes from a Latin word that simply means "flesh."[6] When we live in a carnal manner, we become "fleshly"

6. *Merriam-Webster's Collegiate Dictionary*, 10th ed., see "carnal."

(1 Cor. 3:3). Carnal Christians preoccupy themselves with material, fleshly, worldly pursuits. Instead of receiving the solid "meat" of the Word so they can grow, they remain like babies, drinking only "milk." They have not learned to follow the Spirit's leading, and they fail to guard themselves against the temptations of the flesh.

As Christians, we are to reflect the fruit of the Spirit as listed in Galatians 5:22–23:

> But the fruit of the Spirit is love, joy, peace, patience, kindness, goodness, faithfulness, gentleness, self-control; against such things there is no law.

In contrast, carnal believers often display more "deeds of the flesh" than fruit of the Spirit. These destructive sin patterns are described in verses 19–21:

> Now the deeds of the flesh are evident, which are: immorality, impurity, sensuality, idolatry, sorcery, enmities, strife, jealousy, outbursts of anger, disputes, dissensions, factions, envying, drunkenness, carousing, and things like these, of which I forewarn you . . . that those who practice such things will not inherit the kingdom of God.

Four Characteristics of a Carnal Person

None of us wants to become carnal. So how do we avoid straying onto the wrong path? Let's examine four characteristics of the carnal person so we'll be able to recognize the warning signs.

First of all, *the carnal person is a believer.* Paul describes the Corinthians as "saints" and "brothers," yet he also describes them as "carnal." It's clear that, despite their fleshly pursuits, the Corinthians were still Christians. God didn't disown these prodigal sons and daughters just because they wandered away from Him. And He won't disown us, either! But His desire is for us to glorify Him with our lives. He wants to see us grow in our faith to become mature followers of Christ.

Second, *the carnal person resembles a non-Christian.* He or she is a believer who, from the outside, appears to be lost. The carnal person lacks maturity and usually fails to show evidence of spiritual growth. Every Christian is called to be a light to the world, but it's often hard to see the light shining in this person's life. Most likely, he or she will appear to be more interested in worldly pursuits than in God's kingdom.

Third, *the carnal person is preoccupied with people*. He or she tends to focus on horizontal relationships instead of his or her relationship with God. The carnal Christian spends a great deal of time pursuing his or her relationships, personal agenda, goals, and priorities. This type of person is likely to have an unhealthy dependency on friendships and other relationships.

Fourth, *the carnal person lacks spiritual growth*. Once we become Christians, God wants us to grow. But a carnal person fails to make choices that allow him or her to become more mature. Instead of reading God's Word, praying, seeking accountability, and reaching out to minister to others, the carnal Christian remains self-focused. He or she is capable of and responsible for demonstrating greater wisdom and maturity in his or her behavior.

God calls us to read His Word, to pray, to fellowship with other believers, and to serve within the body of Christ according to our giftedness. When we fail to maintain the spiritual disciplines and begin to disconnect from a local church body, we start to take steps down the dangerous path to carnality.

A Look in the Mirror

It's easy to think of others we know who struggle with carnality. But the first place to look for warning signs is in our own mirror. Ask yourself the following questions: Am I really growing spiritually? Am I connected to a church body? Do I tend to focus more on God or on myself? Am I consumed by my relationships with other people? Does my life clearly radiate the light of Christ, or am I seeing some of the fleshly manifestations of a carnal lifestyle?

Remember Paul's battle? The war between the flesh and the Spirit continues to rage within us, but God has won the final victory. When we confess our sins to the Lord and give Him control of our hearts and lives, we gain power through the Holy Spirit to avoid the pitfalls of carnality.

 Living Insights

As we looked in the mirror, we may have seen the face of carnality staring back at us. How do we know if we have started down that path? And if we have, how do we find our way back to true fellowship with God? To help us pinpoint our "trouble spots," let's address four ways that carnality can express itself in our lives.

Activities

Think about how you spend your time. Are you consistent about maintaining the spiritual disciplines of Bible reading and prayer? Are you actively involved in a church body, or are you a pew-sitter? If you don't feel connected with your local church, list some ministries that you could join. If you are not connected with a church right now, what steps can you take to find one and get involved?

_____

_____

_____

_____

_____

Attitudes

What are your attitudes toward God and other people? Often, when we start down the path to sin, our attitudes about spiritual matters begin to change. We can become closed off from others when we know that we aren't walking closely with the Lord. These hurtful feelings can be masked by anger and a desire to push away those who are trying to hold us accountable. But God calls us to humbly confess our sins and to accept loving correction from others who hold us to God's standard.

Are there any attitudes in your life that could use an adjustment? If so, what are they? Is there anyone in your life whom you need to approach to ask for forgiveness?

_____

_____

_____

_____

_____

Associations

Paul warned the Corinthian believers not to associate with other Christians who lived in a carnal manner. Those with whom we spend our time help shape our character, whether we realize it or not. If we associate with positive, godly people, we will be inspired to be positive and godly. If we associate with angry, negative people, we will tend to become angry and negative. If we spend time with those who are involved with sinful or illicit activities, we will be tempted to become involved in those activities ourselves. Remember: "Bad company corrupts good morals" (1 Cor. 15:33).

Are you currently associating with people who may have a negative influence on you? If so, list some places you might be able to go or resources you could use to meet some godly Christian friends. Name some people you admire or who have a positive influence on you. What steps can you take to get to know them better and spend more time with them?

_____

_____

_____

_____

_____

Appetites

All of us struggle with fleshly appetites and sinful tendencies in particular areas of our lives. What are your struggles right now? Are you drawn toward any activities that you feel are not glorifying to God? If so, take time to confess these activities to God. Below, list some practical ways you can avoid these pitfalls in the future. Name one person you can ask to keep you accountable in this area.

_____

_____

_____

_____

Through the Holy Spirit's presence in our lives, we have the power to win the battle against the flesh. Take the steps to eliminate the darkness of carnality from your life. When you do, you will begin to see the light of God's love working in miraculous new ways!

Chapter 6

LOOKING WITHIN:
ALLOWING GRACE TO
FLOW FREELY

Romans 14:1–19

During the United States' 1988 presidential election, an unexpected shift of attention occurred in the news media. TV stations, radio stations, and newspapers offered extensive coverage of the plight of three gray whales that were cut off from their migratory route by a frozen sea of ice.

At first, only a few people tried to free the trapped whales. But once the media brought the whales' plight into our living rooms, many volunteers flocked to the scene with heavy machinery and steel determination. They vowed to do whatever it took to set the stranded whales free. Americans remained glued to their TV sets, waiting breathlessly to hear any news of the whales' movement toward freedom.

The volunteers worked hard, but they weren't able to make much progress, and their ingenuity and energy were eventually exhausted. So the National Guard came to the rescue, using helicopters to drop a five-ton piece of concrete onto the ice to break it up. Then, in a cooperative effort with the United States, the Soviet Union dispatched two ice-breaking ships to facilitate the rescue. Finally, after three weeks and an expenditure of $1.5 million, the whales were freed. The heroic and noble rescue of these three whales sparked a sense of compassion throughout the world.

If we are willing to go to such lengths to save our ocean-dwelling friends, how much more wholeheartedly should we invest in the lives of people around us! As Christians, we are called to help meet the needs of those outside the family of God as well as to minister to other believers. Every day we have opportunities to help set

---

This chapter has been adapted from the chapters "Guiding Others to Freedom" and "The Grace to Let Others Be" in the Bible study guide *The Grace Awakening*, written by Ken Gire, from the Bible-teaching ministry of Charles R. Swindoll (Anaheim, Calif.: Insight for Living, 1990), pp. 58–77.

others free! Many Christians spend their lives in a cold prison, trapped in the ice of other people's expectations, legalistic requirements, and performance. You may know some believers who have never experienced the *real* freedom guaranteed by Christ's sacrificial love. But you can be part of the answer! Your ministry can help loose other Christians from the chains of legalism.

Let Grace Flow Freely

In order to break the chains of legalism from ourselves and others, we must let grace flow freely. How? First of all, be yourself! And allow others to be who God made them to be. Let them look and dress differently from you if they wish. Let them act differently. Allow them to see things another way. Consider their viewpoints. Don't bend on the essentials of the Gospel, but be open-minded regarding the non-essentials. Allowing grace to flow freely means we let others be. We're satisfied with the way God made others, and we enjoy the ways they differ from us.

Obstacles to Grace

Unfortunately, two strong human tendencies tend to interfere with the principle of letting grace flow. First, we often compare ourselves with others, which leads us to compete with them. Second, we attempt to control others, which results in manipulation. Let's examine these two tendencies that can keep grace from brightening our lives.

Comparing Ourselves to Others

Most people tend to prefer associating with others with similar tastes, comparable attitudes and actions, and common interests. As a result, if someone thinks differently from us, prefers other entertainment, wears a different style of clothing, or enjoys a different lifestyle, we get a little nervous. For instance, how would you respond to a close Christian friend who:

- Plays cards

- Goes out dancing on the weekends

- Listens to secular music

- Goes to the beach one Sunday instead of going to church

- Drives a luxury car
- Owns a second home
- Has a glass of wine with dinner occasionally
- Doesn't have a quiet time in the morning
- Watches certain movies or television shows
- Spends a lot of time with non-Christian friends

These are "gray areas"—areas that the Bible doesn't specifically discuss. Believe it or not, Scripture does not pass moral judgments on these issues. So, if the Bible refuses to comment on such things, why do we? Often, we tend to place too much value upon external attributes and how things look from the outside. We judge by appearances rather than actualities. But we must remember that "God sees not as man sees, for man looks at the outward appearance, but the Lord looks at the heart" (1 Sam. 16:7b).

God never meant for the church to be a religious factory, churning out cookie-cutter Christians and paper-doll saints. On the contrary, He created the church to be a celebration of diversity (see 1 Cor. 12). We are called to appreciate and edify one another as we serve the body of Christ with our unique gifts.

People who struggle with legalism often have difficulty accepting diversity within the body. They tend to assume that all believers must be alike, unified in convictions and uniform in appearance. But grace thinks outside the box. Gracious people find pleasure in diversity, encourage individuality, and leave room for differences of opinion. For us to demonstrate true grace to others, we'll have to let go of the legalistic tendency to compare.

Controlling Others

Another attitude we may struggle with is the desire to control others. This tendency is especially prevalent among those who find their security in legalistic rules or religious rituals. Controlling people manipulate others, using subtle fear tactics, veiled threats, or hints to get their way, and they usually win by intimidating others. And whatever the method, controlling, like comparing, nullifies grace.

Some Biblical Guidelines That Magnify Grace

We want to be able to recognize the warning signs of legalism, but we don't want to dwell on those things that nullify grace.

Instead, we want to discover what magnifies it! In Romans 14, Paul sets forth four practical guidelines to help us offer God's grace to others.

Accept Others

> Now accept the one who is weak in faith, but not for the purpose of passing judgment on his opinions. One person has faith that he may eat all things, but he who is weak eats vegetables only. The one who eats is not to regard with contempt the one who does not eat, and the one who does not eat is not to judge him who eats, for God has accepted him. Who are you to judge the servant of another? To his own master he stands or falls; and he will stand, for the Lord is able to make him stand. (Rom. 14:1–4)

First, we must realize that *accepting others is basic to letting them be*. The problem described in Romans 14 was not entirely a food problem. It was also a problem concerning love for the individual. How often do we restrict our love by making it conditional? How often do we make our acceptance dependent upon how others measure up to our expectations? But whether the subject is the meat sacrificed in a heathen temple or the movie showing in a theater, the principle is the same: Accept one another.

When we don't accept one another, conflicts inevitably arise. The apostle Paul pinpoints the two most common ways that people react to these conflicts. First, he says, "The one who eats is not to regard with contempt the one who does not eat" (v. 3a). The words "regard with contempt" mean to look down on, despise or reject.[1] Second, Paul says, "The one who does not eat is not to judge him who eats" (v. 3b). The word "judge" means "to form a negative opinion about."[2]

No matter how strongly we may feel about a certain cultural taboo, we aren't to judge another who disagrees with us. Why? Because, as verse 4 indicates, other people's convictions regarding the non-essentials of the faith may vary from ours. It's God's job to direct them; it's our job to accept them! Acceptance is basic to

---

1. John F. Walvoord and Roy B. Zuck, eds., *The Bible Knowledge Commentary*, New Testament ed. (Wheaton, Ill.: Victor Books, 1989), p. 492.

2. *Merriam-Webster's Collegiate Dictionary*, 10th ed., see "judge."

letting others be themselves. Consider the next four verses of Romans 14 as we turn to a second guideline.

Let Others Decide for Themselves

> One person regards one day above another, another regards every day alike. Each person must be fully convinced in his own mind. He who observes the day, observes it for the Lord, and he who eats, does so for the Lord, for he gives thanks to God; and he who eats not, for the Lord he does not eat, and gives thanks to God. For not one of us lives for himself, and not one dies for himself; for if we live, we live for the Lord, or if we die, we die for the Lord; therefore whether we live or die, we are the Lord's. (vv. 5–8)

According to this principle, *refusing to dictate to others allows the Lord freedom to direct their lives.* Do you want to help others grow to maturity? Here's how: offer them freedom to grow up differently. Let them blossom at their own pace and in their own way. Let them decide for themselves. Let them have the freedom to fail and learn from their own mistakes.

Paul states in verse 8 that each of us belongs to the Lord. When we realize this, we will stop dictating and start trusting the Lord to direct the steps of His children.

Refuse to Judge Others

The third guideline is found in verses 9–12:

> For to this end Christ died and lived again, that He might be Lord both of the dead and of the living. But you, why do you judge your brother? Or you again, why do you regard your brother with contempt? For we will all stand before the judgment seat of God. For it is written,
> "As I live, says the Lord, every knee shall bow to Me,
> And every tongue shall give praise to God."
> So then each one of us will give account of himself to God.

Freeing others means we never assume a position we're not qualified to fill. What keeps us from being qualified to judge? We aren't omniscient—we don't know all the facts. We're unable to see into people's hearts, so we can't read their motives. We're finite, so we can't see "the big picture." We live with blind spots and blurred perspectives. Most of all, being human, we are imperfect, inconsistent, and subjective.

Does God's command that we are not to judge mean we must always agree with each other? Certainly not. But it does mean we should be civil in our disagreements and extend grace to others.

Express Your Liberty Wisely

The final guideline flows out of verses 13–18:

> Therefore let us not judge one another anymore, but rather determine this—not to put an obstacle or a stumbling block in a brother's way. I know and am convinced in the Lord Jesus that nothing is unclean in itself; but to him who thinks anything to be unclean, to him it is unclean. For if because of food your brother is hurt, you are no longer walking according to love. Do not destroy with your food him for whom Christ died. Therefore do not let what is for you a good thing be spoken of as evil; for the kingdom of God is not eating and drinking, but righteousness and peace and joy in the Holy Spirit. For he who in this way serves Christ is acceptable to God and approved by men.

According to this passage, *loving others requires us to express our liberty wisely*. Because Jesus paid the penalty for our sins, God holds us blameless! "Through regeneration and sanctification the bondage of sin is completely destroyed."[3] We are no longer bound to a set of rules—we have liberty in Christ. Our ultimate goal is not to please ourselves or others, but the Lord (2 Cor. 5:9, 15). One way to show our love for others is by expressing our liberty wisely. We do that by enjoying our liberty without flaunting it . . . quietly, privately, and with those of like mind who aren't offended by the expression of our freedom.

3. Merrill F. Unger, *The New Unger's Bible Dictionary* (Chicago, Ill.: Moody Press, 1998), p. 444.

A Few Actions That Signify Grace

Consider some actions that signify grace:

So then we pursue the things which make for peace
and the building up of one another.

Let's examine two principles gleaned from this statement.

1. Concentrate on things that encourage peace and assist others' growth. Filter whatever you do through this twofold grid: Is this going to encourage peace? Is this going to hurt and offend or help and strengthen?

2. Remember that when we sabotage saints, we hinder the work of God. Paul warns us in verse 20, "Do not tear down the work of God for the sake of food." Be discreet, and don't flaunt your liberty if you know that others have convictions against it.

Determine where you stand on important issues, but offer grace to others who may feel differently. By letting others be themselves, you free yourself to give full attention to what God is doing in your own life!

 Living Insights

To "Let Go" Takes Love

To "let go" does not mean to stop caring, it
means that I can't do it for someone else.
To "let go" is not to cut myself off, it is the
realization that I can't control another.
To "let go" is not to enable, but to allow learning
from natural consequences.
To "let go" is to admit powerlessness, which
means the outcome is not in my hands.
To "let go" is not to try to change or blame
another, it is to make the most of myself.
To "let go" is not to care for, but to care about.
To "let go" is not to fix, but to be supportive.
To "let go" is not to judge, but to allow another to
be a human being.
To "let go" is not to be in the middle arranging

all the outcomes but to allow others to effect
their own destinies.
To "let go" is not to be protective, it is to permit
another to face reality.
To "let go" is not to deny, but to accept.
To "let go" is not to nag, scold, or argue, but
instead to search out my own shortcomings
and to correct them.
To "let go" is not to adjust everything to my
desires but to take each day as it comes, and
to cherish myself in it.
To "let go" is not to criticize and regulate anybody
but to try to become what I dream
I can be.
To "let go" is not to regret the past, but to grow
and to live for the future.
To "let go" is to fear less and to love more.[4]

Turn this poem into a prayer list for your personal needs. You
may want to begin your prayer something like this: "Dear Lord, please
teach me how to let go . . ." Record your petition to God here.

_____

_____

_____

_____

_____

_____

Now, take your prayer a step further by making it more specific.
Take several lines of the poem and apply them to your life. For
example, you might apply the first line to someone to whom you're
having a hard time giving freedom. Your prayer might be: "Lord,
help me let go of _____. I know I'm crowding

4. "To 'Let Go' Takes Love," quoted by Margaret J. Rinck in *Can Christians Love Too Much?*
(Grand Rapids, Mich.: Zondervan Publishing House, Pyranee Books, 1989), p. 157. Refer-
enced in the Bible study guide *The Grace Awakening,* written by Ken Gire, from the Bible-
teaching ministry of Charles R. Swindoll (Anaheim, Calif.: Insight for Living, 1990),
p. 64–65.

_____'s life and trespassing in areas that I shouldn't be. Help me care for _____ in such a way that I don't tread upon his or her self-respect. Specifically, Lord, help me back away from doing these particular things . . ." Using the verses of the poem as a guide, try to concentrate on several areas, offering them to the Lord.

Thank God for the work He has done in your life, and take time to praise Him for His grace. Release your burdens and your relationships to Him, knowing that only He can break the chains from your life and the lives of those around you. Only He can offer you true freedom through Christ!

Chapter 7

LOOKING AROUND:
BEING A GOOD NEIGHBOR

Luke 10:25–37

Sometimes we need to get back to the basics.

When playing at their zenith, the Green Bay Packers were practically unbeatable. But the team grew overconfident and lost what should have been an easy game against the Chicago Bears on Soldier Field. Naturally, their coach, Vince Lombardi, was livid. When his team's plane returned home to frozen-over Green Bay, Lombardi bused his players directly to Lambeau Field, ordering them to don their still-sweaty gear from the game. Then he sat the players down, held up a pigskin, and announced, "Gentlemen, this is a football!"

How basic can you get? You might as well tell a violinist in the Boston Symphony Orchestra, "This is an eighth note," or inform a librarian, "This is a book." But when we begin to get sidetracked from our goals, we need to return to the basics. It's the same with our faith. And for Christians, that means caring for our neighbors.

Just as a player knows football, a violinist knows eighth notes, and a librarian knows books, we're expected to know what it means to be a good neighbor. And we're also expected to *act* on that knowledge. How can we honestly say we're interested in reaching the world for Christ if we're not concerned with reaching the family next door? Or our colleague in the office across the hall? Or the college student working at the coffee shop we visit each morning?

Let's take a closer look at our neighbors: those we connect with every day, those we meet grilling hamburgers in the backyard, making copies across the hall, and standing in line waiting for a latté. We'll start by joining our "Head Coach" in Luke 10, where

This chapter has been adapted from "What About My Neighbor's Neighbor?" in the Bible study guide *The Continuation of Something Great: Jesus' Teaching and Training of the Disciples*, written by Bryce Klabunde, from the Bible-teaching ministry of Charles R. Swindoll (Fullerton, Calif.: Insight for Living, 1995), pp. 130–137, and from "Is My Neighbor Really Lost?" in the Bible study guide *Questions Christians Ask*, written by David Lein, from the Bible-teaching ministry of Charles R. Swindoll (Fullerton, Calif.: Insight for Living, 1989), pp. 34–38.

Jesus got back to the basics by announcing: "Christian, this is what it means to be a true neighbor!"

Addressing the Heart of the Issue

Rather than preach a sermon on being a good neighbor, Jesus masterfully illustrated neighborliness for us in the moving story of the Good Samaritan. He told this parable in the context of a conversation He had with a Jewish lawyer who had decided to put Jesus to the test.

A Dialogue between a Lawyer and Jesus

The legal expert began by asking a question:

> And a lawyer stood up and put Him to the test, saying, "Teacher, what shall I do to inherit eternal life?" (Luke 10:25)

Turning the tables on the man, Jesus answered with another question:

> "What is written in the Law? How does it read to you?" (v. 26)

William Barclay points out the subtlety in Jesus' response:

> Strict orthodox Jews wore round their wrists little leather boxes called phylacteries, which contained certain passages of scripture—Exodus 13:1–10; 11–16; Deuteronomy 6:4–9; 11:13–20. So Jesus said to the scribe, "Look at the phylactery on your own wrist and it will answer your question."[1]

Dutifully, the lawyer quoted the Scripture he knew so well:

> "You shall love the Lord your God with all your heart, and with all your soul, and with all your strength, and with all your mind; and your neighbor as yourself." (Luke 10:27)

Jesus congratulated him for giving the right answer, but He also

---

1. William Barclay, *The Gospel of Luke*, rev. ed., The Daily Study Bible Series (Philadelphia, Penn.: Westminster Press, 1975), p. 140.

challenged him to go beyond Scripture memory and start putting his knowledge into action:

> And He said to him, "You have answered correctly;
> do this and you will live." (v. 28)

Essentially, Jesus told the lawyer, "You have the right idea. So do something about it!" As far as Jesus was concerned, the case was closed. The lawyer, however, didn't care for this incriminating verdict. Reluctant to leave the scene, he shifted the argument back to Jesus and tried to get off the hook by quibbling over the meaning of a word:

> But wishing to justify himself, he said to Jesus, "And
> who is my neighbor?" (v. 29)

Some rabbis of the day, according to Barclay, "confined the word neighbour to their fellow Jews."[2] But Jesus sidestepped this issue by telling a story that would explain His meaning beyond a doubt.

Jesus Tells a Story

> Jesus replied and said, "A man was going down from
> Jerusalem to Jericho, and fell among robbers, and
> they stripped him and beat him, and went away leav-
> ing him half dead." (Luke 10:30)

Jesus' story is about a man in need—a man who had taken a treacherous journey from Jerusalem to Jericho, where the way was craggy and steep and the altitude dropped thirty-six hundred feet over a distance of twenty miles. Robbers loved that lonely stretch of road. They could mug and murder travelers there without fear of intervention. Called "The Bloody Way," it was a threatening and dangerous road for a person traveling alone.[3]

As Jesus continued, the drama heightened. He introduced two religious men into His story, drawing the pious lawyer into a net of emotional identification:

> "And by chance a priest was going down on that
> road, and when he saw him, he passed by on the

2. Barclay, *The Gospel of Luke*, p. 140.
3. Barclay, *The Gospel of Luke*, pp. 138–39.

other side. Likewise a Levite also, when he came to the place and saw him, passed by on the other side." (Luke 10:31–32)

These two men deliberately avoided the bleeding man lying crumpled in the dirt. The first was a priest of Jerusalem's temple, a man whose life was consecrated to the things of God. The second, a Levite, was an assistant to the first. Both men, religious professionals, saw the man but ignored the need.

James, the half-brother of Jesus, had something to say about this kind of heartless religion—"It's useless!"

> If a brother or sister is without clothing and in need of daily food, and one of you says to them, "Go in peace, be warmed and be filled," and yet you do not give them what is necessary for their body, what use is that? Even so faith, if it has no works, is dead, being by itself. (James 2:15–17)

And, according to John, if we truly love God, we'll open our hearts and show love toward others also:

> We know love by this, that He laid down His life for us; and we ought to lay down our lives for the brethren. But whoever has the world's goods, and sees his brother in need and closes his heart against him, how does the love of God abide in him? Little children, let us not love with word or with tongue, but in deed and truth. (1 John 3:16–18)

In Jesus' story, He next contrasted the response of the two religious men with that of another traveler—a man with unusual understanding and compassion:

> "But a Samaritan, who was on a journey, came upon him; and when he saw him, he felt compassion, and came to him and bandaged up his wounds, pouring oil and wine on them; and he put him on his own beast, and brought him to an inn and took care of him. On the next day he took out two denarii and gave them to the innkeeper and said, 'Take care of him; and whatever more you spend, when I return, I will repay you.'" (Luke 10:33–35)

Samaritans were Jews whose ancestors came from the northern ten tribes of Israel. The Samaritan people had long ago intermarried with the Assyrians. They also held that Mount Gerizim, not Jerusalem, was the true place of worship. For these reasons, the full-blooded Jews despised the Samaritans and criticized their beliefs. Yet it was a Samaritan whose faith proved him the most worthy neighbor.

Jesus said the Samaritan "felt compassion" (v. 33). This term meant "to be moved as to one's bowels . . . for the bowels were thought to be the seat of love and pity."[4] The Samaritan saw the same pitiful man lying beside the road in agony, and his heart stirred within him so that he couldn't pass by without helping. That's the way compassion affects us. It stirs us; it troubles us; it keeps us awake at night until we do something.

Did you notice the lengths to which the Samaritan went to show love to the man?

• He came to him.

• He poured oil and wine on the man's wounds to disinfect them, and then bandaged them.

• He put the man on his donkey and brought him to an inn.

• He took care of the man through the night.

• The next day, he paid for at least three weeks' worth of lodging and food to ensure the man's full recovery.[5]

Unlike Jerusalem's religious elite, the Samaritan went the extra mile for this man in need. He was a good neighbor—which brought Jesus to the point of His story.

The Characteristics of a True Neighbor

Jesus narrowed His message to a single question, shot like an arrow straight through the lawyer's heart:

"Which of these three do you think proved to be a neighbor to the man who fell into the robbers'

4. James Strong, Enhanced Strong's Lexicon (Ontario: Woodside Bible Fellowship, 1996), see "splagchinizomai," no. 4697, accessed through the Logos Library System.

5. Darrell Bock, "Luke," Volume 2:9:51–24:53, Baker Exegetical Commentary on the New Testament (Grand Rapids, Mich.: Baker Books, 1996), p. 1033.

hands?" And he said, "The one who showed mercy toward him." Then Jesus said to him, "Go and do the same." (Luke 10:36–37)

The poignant parable defies any rebuttal from the lawyer. The Lord deftly shifted from the original question, "Who is my neighbor?" to the more important question, "What kind of neighbor am I?"

Like the lawyer, we tend to want to place the burden of responsibility on someone else's shoulders. Our degree of mercy often depends on whether people fit our description of a "worthy neighbor." But Jesus places the burden of compassion on us. Are we really people who love the Lord our God with all our heart, soul, strength, and mind? Do we truly love our neighbors as ourselves and prove it by our actions?

Coming to Terms with the Truth

The answer to these questions depends on who we are and how much we desire to change. The Samaritan was a compassionate man who sympathized with the wounded man's brokenness and pain. As a result, he did something about it. The principle is this: *Who we are determines what we see, and what we see determines what we do.*

One man writes with conviction,

> Compassion is not a snob gone slumming. . . . Did you ever take a real trip down inside the broken heart of a friend? To feel the sob of the soul—the raw, red crucible of emotional agony? To have this become almost as much yours as that of your soul-crushed neighbor? Then, to sit down with him—and silently weep? This is the beginning of compassion.[6]

Christianity doesn't get more basic than this! A caring, compassionate heart is absolutely essential to the message we have to share with the world. It is God's deep love and Christ's sacrifice for us that we should model for others. It is only through the Holy Spirit that our hearts are changed and our eyes are opened to the needs of those around us. Our neighbors won't understand Christ's love until they see it demonstrated by our outstretched hands.

---

6. Jess Moody, as quoted in *Quotable Quotations*, comp. Lloyd Cory (Wheaton, Ill.: Scripture Press Publications, Victor Books, 1985), p. 76.

How can we demonstrate Christ's love? Charles R. Swindoll illustrates one practical way in a personal story that goes back to his days in seminary.

In his last year at school, several crises caused Chuck to enter a dark period of depression. As you read in chapter two, Chuck's wife, Cynthia, had a miscarriage when she was five-and-a-half months pregnant. Three months later, Chuck's car was hit by a drunk driver. His son's jaw was broken, and Cynthia, who was pregnant again, was injured as well. In the following seven months, Cynthia remained bedridden, in and out of the hospital, threatened with losing another baby. And during all this, her mother was slowly dying of breast cancer in Houston, Texas.

Chuck's family was hurting; he was without money or a car, and he faced an unknown future. He tells what happened one night after the accident while Cynthia was in the hospital, when he was feeling especially low.

> Late one evening, after studying in the library till it closed, I thought I would go find a professor who would put his arms around me, a man I had studied under, someone, any one of them that I had been learning from and following for three and a half years. I remember knocking on a door and no one answered, and walking a little further and no one answered. Finally, there [was] a light on. Somebody [was] there.
>
> And, rather coolly, this man I had known for those years opened his door a crack. "Yes?" he stared at me. And when I saw his face, had I known it was him, I don't believe I would have disturbed him, because I knew when I saw him that he didn't have the capacity to understand. . . .
>
> "Yes, Chuck. What do you want?"
>
> I stood there and tears just ran from my eyes. And I could hear in his voice that he didn't want to talk to me. I said, "Am I disturbing you?"
>
> "Yes, you're disturbing me. What do you want?" was his answer.

I said, "Nothing. I don't want anything."
He said, "Fine." Closed the door.
I needed somebody. I wanted somebody who
would simply understand what it felt like. . . .
The next morning, while still trying to find my
way through the labyrinth of my feelings and get up
on my own feet from my depression and my fears of
losing our baby and maybe even losing a wife—I
didn't know—Howie Hendricks walked up to me
and put his arms around me and won my heart and
has won it to this day. And he understood [my con-
fusion] as he told me of their miscarriage. And then
I wanted to know what he knew, because I then
knew how much he cared.[7]

Showing compassion can be as simple as putting an arm around
someone and sharing their sorrow. All it takes is an ability to see the
signs of pain, stop what we're doing, and open the door wide. How
have you experienced compassion from others when you were hurting?

_____

_____

_____

_____

Has someone been knocking on your door, looking for understanding and compassion? If so, who is it, and what hurts is this
person experiencing right now?

_____

_____

_____

_____

7. From Charles R. Swindoll's sermon, "What about My Neighbor's Neighbor?," given at the
First Evangelical Free Church of Fullerton, California, November 22, 1992.

Take this opportunity to be intentional about your compassion. How can you help this friend or family member in need? How can you be a true neighbor to him or her?

_____

_____

_____

_____

_____

_____

Chapter 8

LOOKING AROUND: CULTIVATING AN APPETITE FOR CHRIST IN OTHERS

Matthew 5:13–16

Quick—name your three closest friends. Are any of them non-Christians? Most likely, they aren't.

Is this how God wants Christians to live? Sometimes we forget that Jesus rubbed shoulders with unbelievers. His dinner guests often looked like they belonged in a police line-up, and He spent much of His time talking with prostitutes, lepers, and other people who were considered complete outcasts in Jewish society. Yet Jesus was a true friend to these people. He had compassion for them. He healed their sicknesses and forgave their sins.

Once we establish a relationship with Christ, we have a tendency to isolate ourselves from the world. We feel called to leave behind the people and things that influenced us before we became Christians. But if we completely isolate ourselves from the world, we risk mistaking a *transformed* life for a *quarantined* life. We're in danger of saturating our schedules with so many church functions that we interact only with other believers. This can hinder us from fulfilling the Great Commission of Christ, which is to "Go therefore and make disciples of all the nations . . ." (Matt. 28:19a).

We can't make an *impact* without making *contact*. Joe Aldrich defines a common view of reaching the lost:

> For many, evangelism is what the pastor does on Sunday morning as he throws the lure over the pulpit, hoping some "fish" in the stained-glass aquarium will bite.[1]

Parts of this chapter have been adapted from "A Simple Counterstrategy: Shake and Shine" in the study guide *Simple Faith*, written by Ken Gire, from the Bible-teaching ministry of Charles R. Swindoll (Plano, Tex.: Insight for Living, 2002), p. 23.

1. Joseph C. Aldrich, *Life-Style Evangelism: Crossing Traditional Boundaries to Reach the Unbelieving World* (Portland, Oreg.: Multnomah Press, 1981), p. 17.

But most of the people who need to establish a relationship with God are not in church on Sunday morning! The most eloquent presentation of the Gospel is not the preacher's sermon—it's how we live from Monday through Saturday. When the accomplished author and professor Sheldon Vanauken wrestled with the claims of Christianity, he wrote the following in his journal:

> The best argument for Christianity is Christians: their joy, their certainty, their completeness. But the strongest argument *against* Christianity is also Christians—when they are sombre and joyless, when they are self-righteous and smug in complacent consecration, when they are narrow and repressive, then Christianity dies a thousand deaths.[2]

We're the only Bible that some people will ever read. They might throw away church flyers and evangelistic tracts without a glance, but when they find out that we're Christians, they will closely analyze our words and actions. They'll read the fine print of our lives to see if the person measures up to the message. They want to see if our walk matches our talk!

Most non-Christian people aren't really looking for perfection, but an absence of hypocrisy. For instance, we as Christians say we believe in the sanctity of marriage. So, when our marriage gets rocky, do we love our spouse unconditionally? Do we support him or her no matter what? Or do we file for a divorce? If we preach about God but live like the world, we seem like fakes. And most people can spot a fake from a mile away.

In the previous chapter, we looked around at our neighbors. Many of them may not know the truth about God, but they know us. They struggle in the same ways we do—working hard to pay the bills, trying to raise their kids, bickering with their spouses. And deep down inside, they long for *connectedness*. They want to be understood and loved. They desire deep friendships and answers to life's tough questions. So let's determine how we, as imperfect people, can help draw them to Christ.

Jesus began His Sermon on the Mount (Matt. 5:3–12) by listing the characteristics of a genuine Christ-follower. And guess what? You won't find perfection among them. But you *will* find meekness,

---

2. Sheldon Vanauken, *A Severe Mercy* (San Francisco, Calif.: HarperSanFrancisco, 1980), p. 85.

spiritual thirst, mercy, purity, peacekeeping, and perseverance—all qualities that reflect the heart, mind, and attitudes of Christ.

As we radiate Christlikeness, we'll have a radical impact on our communities. Though we are not *of* the world, we are *in* the world, seasoning it and illuminating it as the salt and light that God has called us to be.

Be the Salt

"You are the salt of the earth . . ." (Matt. 5:13)

Salt is more than just a condiment on the dinner table. Not only is it "one of the most important substances mentioned in the Bible, but it is a necessity of life."[3] Salt serves four purposes: it cleanses, it preserves, it adds flavor, and it creates thirst.

Salt Cleanses

For thousands of years, salt has been used for cleansing. You may have noticed that when salt is applied to a wound, the wound stings. This stinging sensation results as the salt attacks infection and cleanses the wound of impurities. The ancient Jewish people rubbed their newborn babies with salt, believing the practice cleansed the child (Ezek. 16:4). And the Hebrews sprinkled their sacrifices with salt to signify purity (Ex. 30:35; Lev. 2:13; Ezek. 43:24).[4]

Paul called us "saints" (Rom. 1:7), or "set-apart ones." We are set apart to cleanse and purify an impure world. Commissioned as emissaries of His grace, we have the honor of applying our salt as a healing balm to the wounded hearts of people.

Salt Preserves

Salt also acts as a preservative. Before the days of refrigeration, people used salt to halt the natural decay of food products. In Jesus' time, fish were packed with salt to arrest corruption on the way to market.[5] In the same way, we as Christians act as a preservative in our quickly deteriorating culture.

---

3. Ronald F. Youngblood, ed., *Nelson's New Illustrated Bible Dictionary,* ed. F. F. Bruce, electronic edition of the rev. ed. of *Nelson's Illustrated Bible Dictionary* (Nashville: Thomas Nelson, 1997), see "salt."

4. Youngblood, ed., *Nelson's New Illustrated Bible Dictionary,* see "salt."

5. Stuart Briscoe, *The Sermon on the Mount: Daring to Be Different* (Wheaton, Ill.: Harold Shaw Publishers, 1995), p. 52.

In our post-modern world, non-Christian people often treat truth like food at an all-you-can-eat buffet. They take only what tastes good to them, and they ignore the rest! Without the influence of Christians to serve as its moral compass, our society would be even more desperately off course than it is now. Theologian John Stott points out:

> One can hardly blame unsalted meat for going bad. It cannot do anything else. The real question to ask is: where is the salt?[6]

We rub salt into meat to preserve it. In the same way, we "rub" against others in the world so that we may permeate them with our saltiness. We're called to be set apart and holy. We're exhorted to cling to God's absolutes in the quagmire of relativism. And we're to do it graciously, not self-righteously.

Salt Adds Flavor

Ever been at a table without a saltshaker? It's no fun. Even Job once asked, "Can something tasteless be eaten without salt, or is there any taste in the white of an egg?" (Job 6:6). Just as salt adds flavor to bland food, we as Christians should add zest to life! But unfortunately, many Christians are as bland as unsalted egg whites. Their lives are defined more by what they *can't* do than what they *can*. Jesus warned us of falling into such a trap when He said,

> ". . . but if the salt has become tasteless, how can it be made salty again?[7] It is no longer good for anything, except to be thrown out and trampled under foot by men." (Matt. 5:13b)

When we lose our zest, we lose our effectiveness. Stuart Briscoe says, "We Christians have no business being boring. Our function is to add flavor and excitement."[8] Isn't that great? Jesus left people

---

6. John R. W. Stott, *The Message of The Sermon on the Mount* (Matthew 5–7), rev. ed. of *Christian Counter-Culture* (Downers Grove, Ill.: InterVarsity Press, 1978), p. 65.

7. Technically, sodium chloride, or salt, cannot disintegrate. However, much of the salt used in the ancient Near East in Jesus' day was taken from the Dead Sea. Such salt was contaminated by other minerals and could be dissolved out of the mixture, leaving a tasteless substance. *International Standard Bible Encyclopedia*, vol. 4: Q–Z, ed. Geoffrey W. Bromiley (Grand Rapids, Mich.: William B. Eerdmans Publishing Company, 1988), p. 287.

8. Briscoe, *The Sermon on the Mount*, p. 55.

wanting more. He left them hungering for His words, hoping for His touch, and more than that, thirsty for the living water that only He could provide.

Salt Creates Thirst

Salt creates a thirst in us. When Christ interacted with people, He "salted" their lives, leaving them longing for His eternal springs. In her book *Out of the Saltshaker and into the World*, Rebecca Pippert said,

> A friend of mine has said that he always discovered a lot about a person when he knew who liked the person and who did not. In Jesus' case, we have the story of the holiest man who ever lived, and yet it was the prostitutes and lepers and thieves who adored him, and the religious who hated his guts.[9]

Do we make others thirsty for Christ? When people are around us, do their parched souls pant for the water of life that they see flowing in our demeanor, our character, and our attitudes? Remember—Jesus didn't give us the option to be salt. He said, "You are the salt"! Don't lose your taste. Instead, seek to be a cleansing preservative, adding flavor and creating thirst in a spiritually bland culture.

Be the Light

"You are the light of the world." (Matt. 5:14a)

The world without Christ is as dark as a sky devoid of stars. In the midst of such moral and spiritual blackness, Jesus calls us "the light." Light serves three purposes in our lives: it attracts attention, it gives hope, and it dispels darkness.

Light Attracts Attention

"A city set on a hill cannot be hidden . . ." (Matt. 5:14b)

In the dark Palestinian night, the fires of Jerusalem blazed to guide weary travelers toward the city. Picture a young man on a

9. Rebecca Manley Pippert, *Out of the Saltshaker and into the World: Evangelism as a Way of Life* (Downers Grove, Ill.: InterVarsity Press, 1979), p. 39.

lonely country road at night, the clouds blotting out every star. Sleep tugs at his eyelids, but the thought of bandits hiding in the shadows keeps him pressing on. Suddenly he reaches a hilltop, and his soul floods with relief at the sight of the flickering fires of Jerusalem. Like these beckoning blazes, we should attract lost and weary wanderers with the light of Christ.

Light Gives Hope

As light, we offer hope to a hopeless generation. Jesus has commissioned us to carry the torch of His love back into our dark world. But unfortunately, many of us only turn on our lights in the safe company of fellow believers. We bask in the brightness of close fellowship, while the world sees only a tiny sliver of light peeking out from under our closed church doors. When we do this, we're burying our lamps under a basket:

> "Nor does anyone light a lamp and put it under a basket, but on the lampstand, and it gives light to all who are in the house." (Matt. 5:15)

No one turns on a flashlight in the noonday sun. It's only necessary when we're surrounded by darkness! Since we as Christians already have the light, let's take the Gospel to those who need hope, to those who are still wandering in the dark.

Light Dispels Darkness

Not only does light attract attention and give hope, but it also dispels darkness. In a spiritual sense, parts of this world are like the bowels of a deep cavern, where the darkness is so impenetrable that people can't even see their hands in front of their faces. There, they experience not just a loss of vision, but a loss of direction.

The only remedy for such disorientation is *light*. One lit match can dispel a whole expanse of darkness. When light appears, circumstances become illuminated, and hope returns as lost people discover their way out of the cave. And once they have found their way out, they're called to help others do the same.

It's comforting to know that no darkness is so thick that Christ's powerful light cannot penetrate it. The Torch that came into the world at the Incarnation, and whose light has been handed down from generation to generation of believers, cannot be hidden (John 1:4–5; 8:12; 9:5).

When our salt is flavorful and our light is radiant, people take notice:

> "Let your light shine before men in such a way that they may see your good works, and glorify your Father who is in heaven." (Matt. 5:16)

Notice that our light is not made up of our words, our beliefs, or our preaching. While these things are essential, Jesus stated that it's our good works that attract people to God. If our churches closed up shop tomorrow, would our communities notice a difference? Do others know us more by our lists of rules or by our works of service? People need to know that we care about them. As we stated earlier, non-Christians can spot a fake a mile away, but they can also spot the true light. And God can use its glow to illuminate even the most darkened hearts.

How to Be Salt and Light

Christ calls us all to shake our salt into the world. To shine our light. To minister to the individuals around us who are hurting. To be a city on a hill that shines for years to come. In order for us to maximize our saltiness and our brightness, here are four applications:

Live right and start praying. In your character, be pure; in your culture, be relevant. Authentically pursue holiness. Seek the Spirit's direction. Be equipped with evangelistic tools, but also be sensitive to the Spirit's prompting. And remember, the prayers of the righteous accomplish much!

Care about and reach out. Start by being friendly. Do you know your neighbors' names? Their children's ages? Do you minister to hurting friends and coworkers? Do you pray with others in times of crisis? Instead of being "spoiled" by your family of believers, work on extending some grace and spreading some salt beyond your church walls.

Be available and listen. As you pray and care for your non-Christian friends, they will respond. People will come to you when they realize that you care. After a while, your door might need a new knocker! So be prepared to offer some genuine Christian hospitality. Remember that what may seem at first to be interruptions may actually be divine appointments for you to share Christ.

Share openly and follow through. For three years, Jesus poured His life into people. With words, deeds, and attitudes, He embodied the

Gospel. In contrast, we often strive to do good deeds but fall short of truly communicating the life-changing Gospel to others. We care, but we resist crossing that invisible barrier to actually share Christ. How shameful if we only shine our light inside the church! When the Spirit leads, pick up your saltshaker and light your lamp.

When you start to apply these four simple principles, sharing your salt and light with others, don't be surprised if your parties start to attract a different crowd. Who knows, people at your church might even start labeling you a "friend of sinners." What a great title!

⚜ *Living Insights*

Saint Francis of Assisi once said, "Preach the Gospel always; and when necessary, use words." [10] Jesus acted out the Gospel, merging truth with proof of God's love. And so did the early Christians. The Roman world sat stunned at these loving, caring, socially conscious believers in Christ. More than being evangelistically bold, these believers reached out to help meet real needs.

Between A.D. 165 and 251, two plagues decimated a third of the Roman Empire. While most people ran from those afflicted with the plague, the exhortations of the Gospel propelled believers to action:

> The willingness of Christians to care for others was put on dramatic public display. . . . Pagans tried to avoid all contact with the afflicted, often casting the still-living into the gutters. Christians, on the other hand, nursed the sick, even though [some] died doing so. . . . Christians also were visible and valuable during the frequent natural and social disasters afflicting the Greco-Roman world: earthquakes, famines, floods, riots, civil wars, and invasions. Even in healthier times, the pagan emperor, Julian, noted the followers of The Way "support not only their poor, *but ours* as well." [11]

10. Saint Francis of Assisi, as quoted by Thomas H. Jeavons and Rebekah Burch Basinger in *Growing Givers' Hearts: Treating Fundraising as Ministry* (San Francisco, Calif.: Jossey-Bass Publishers, 2000), p. 17.

11. Rodney Stark, as quoted by Robert Lewis and Rob Wilkins in *The Church of Irresistible Influence* (Grand Rapids, Mich.: Zondervan Publishing House, 2001), p. 45.

What if the world knew us more by our good works than just our good words? Reflect on the following verses. How do they encourage us to live out the Gospel?

Romans 12:20–21 _____

_____

_____

_____

Galatians 6:9–10 _____

_____

_____

_____

1 Timothy 6:17–19 _____

_____

_____

Titus 3:8 _____

_____

_____

_____

If we fall in love with the truth of the Gospel without providing proof of our faith, we miss our divine calling to be salt and light to a desperate world. So sieze every opportunity to shake and shine!

BOOKS FOR
PROBING FURTHER

We hope that you've gained a fresh perspective on your spiritual walk as you have studied this guide. We encourage you to continue on the path of becoming salt and light by investigating some additional resources. You'll be challenged to grow and mature in your faith as you dig into these books to discover the treasures they contain. These resources will help you "shake and shine" as they encourage you to add flavor and brightness to the world around you!

Bailey, Ney. *Faith Is Not a Feeling*. Colorado Springs, Colo.: Water-Brook Press, 2002.

Crabb, Larry and Dan B. Allender. *Hope When You're Hurting*. Grand Rapids, Mich.: Zondervan Publishing House, 1996.

Dillow, Linda and Lorraine Pintus. *Intimate Issues: Conversations Woman to Woman*. Colorado Springs, Colo.: WaterBrook Press, 1999.

Foster, Richard J. *A Celebration of Discipline*. San Francisco, Calif.: Harper Books, 1988.

Lewis, Robert with Rob Wilkins. *The Church of Irresistible Influence*. Grand Rapids, Mich.: Zondervan Publishing House, 2001.

Lutzer, Erwin W. *How to Say No to a Stubborn Habit When You Really Want to Say Yes*. Colorado Springs, Colo.: Chariot Victor Press, 1994.

Mabery-Foster, Lucy. *Women and the Church: Reaching, Teaching, and Developing Women for Christ*. Nashville, Tenn.: Word Publishing, 1999.

Moore, Beth. *Breaking Free: Making Liberty in Christ a Reality in Life*. Nashville, Tenn.: Broadman and Holman Publishers, 2000.

———. *Praying God's Word: Breaking Free from Spiritual Strongholds*. Nashville, Tenn.: Broadman and Holman Publishers, 2000.

Patterson, Ben. *Deepening Your Conversation with God: Learning to Love to Pray*. Minneapolis, Minn.: Bethany House Publishers, 2001.

Swindoll, Charles R. *Flying Closer to the Flame: A Passion for the Holy Spirit*. Dallas, Tex.: Word Publishing, 1993.

———. *Living above the Level of Mediocrity: A Commitment to Excellence*. Dallas, Tex.: Word Publishing, 1989.

Worthington, Everett. *Five Steps to Forgiveness: The Art and Science of Forgiving*. New York, N.Y.: Crown Publishers, 2001.

Yancey, Philip. *Church: Why Bother?* Grand Rapids, Mich.: Zondervan Publishing House, 1998.

———. *Disappointment with God*. Grand Rapids, Mich.: Zondervan Publishing House, 1988.

———. *What's So Amazing About Grace?* Grand Rapids, Mich.: Zondervan Publishing House, 1997.

———. *Where Is God When It Hurts?* Grand Rapids, Mich: Zondervan Publishing House, 1997.

Some of the books listed may be out of print and available only through a library. For those currently available, please contact your local Christian bookstore. Books by Charles R. Swindoll and many books by other authors may be obtained through the Insight for Living Resource Center.

Insight for Living also has Bible study guides available on many books of the Bible as well as on a variety of topics, Bible characters, and contemporary issues. For more information, see the ordering instructions that follow and contact the office that serves you.